America Remembered

Handwritten inscription: To Anita — Enjoy this blend of fellow Americans — there's even a bit of mystery and intrigue

Christian Authors Guild Writers
Showcase Reflections of America

Handwritten: God Bless America!

COMPILED AND EDITED BY

LYNN B. PUGH

(signature: Lynn)

Vineyard Sound Books
Dartmouth, Massachusetts

Y0-DLB-164

©2010 Lynn B. Pugh

All rights reserved. No part of this publication may be reproduced, stored in a retrieval system, or transmitted in any form or by any means—electronic, mechanical, photocopying, recording, or otherwise—without the prior written permission of the publisher. The only exception is brief quotations in printed reviews.

Published by Vineyard Sound Books
370 Fisher Road
Dartmouth, MA 02747
www.VineyardSoundBooks.com

Printed in the United States of America

Compiled and Edited by Lynn B. Pugh

Photos used with permission, Bill Birch

Cover by Monica Ann Luzzo-Moyer

Library of Congress Cataloging-in-Publication Data

Pugh, Lynn B., 1960-
    America Remembered / Lynn B. Pugh

Patriotism / Christian Life / Inspiration
ISBN: 978-0-9825075-4-4

*What's more American than
hot dogs, baseball, and apple pie?*

*From majestic mountains to shining seas,
the unequivocal answer is, of course, you!*

America Remembered is dedicated to everyone who preserves this beautiful land and the ideals of our great country.

Within these pages, you will find hidden treasures that may surprise and delight you. Look back with us as we offer a tribute to our heritage, and ahead, as we share words of hope for the future.

Thirty-three authors of the Christian Authors Guild share remembrances from the foundations of our nation to blessings for our emerging generations. Included are writing samples from our talented pool of first published to our highly celebrated award-winning authors.

Our humor with heart for America is woven through this book like a golden thread of unity. Be entertained by our variety of styles from fiction to nonfiction, from regional colloquialism to poetry.

*We hope you'll agree,
This land is made for you and me!*

Christian Authors Guild is celebrating our 10th anniversary with this new release. Our group has written together since 2000 in our official monthly newsletter, *The Wave*, and our previous four books: *Stepping Stones Across the Stream of Time* (2003), *The Desk in the Attic* (2004), *No Small Miracles* (2005), and *Heartfelt Inspirations* (2008).

The growing membership of the Christian Authors Guild meets twice monthly. We share writing and speaking tips, encourage growth through critique groups, host writing events, and enjoy Christian fellowship.

Monthly speakers, Coffee & Quill writing seminar, and our Annual Catch the Wave Writers Conference are only a few benefits of membership. There are year-round opportunities to serve on leadership teams and committees, and many participate in our writing contests.

To reach our authors:
Info@ChristianAuthorsGuild.org

Please visit our Web site today:
www.ChristianAuthorsGuild.org

Thank you for purchasing a copy of our newest inspirational publication, *America Remembered*.

ACKNOWLEDGMENTS

The Christian Authors Guild, established in 2000, consists of a growing membership of gifted writers. God blesses our work and leads us as we journey together, sending out a Christian wave upon a secular sea. Thank you to all members and leaders, past and present, for your excellent work and commitment to our purpose.

Unified, we offer praise, honor, and glory to God for bringing *America Remembered* to publication.

Special recognition to these Christian Authors Guild members for their contribution of time and talent:

>Bill Larmore, Lloyd Blackwell, Diana Baker, Mary Bowen, Mike Anderson, and Martha Ureke.

For keeping the wind in my sails, my deepest gratitude to my amazing husband, Rick Pugh, my talented dad, Bill Birch, and my dear friend and publisher, Stephen Caravana.

To friends, spiritual advisors, and mentors across America who so generously gave encouragement and support—*Thank you for everything!*

~ Lynn B. Pugh

CONTENTS

From early dates in America to the future,
PLEASE ENJOY:

America's Symbol of Hope
    by Jack Elder..........................1
A Lasting Legacy
    by Charlene C. Elder..................7
Wave Upon Wave They Came
    by Nadine Blyseth....................14
Freedom and Opportunities Ring
    by Susan M. Watkins.................17
The Letter
    by Patty Rocco.......................24
Freedom to Build
    by Cynthia L. Simmons..............31
Aloha
    by Bonnie Greenwood Grant.......36
The Way it Was
    by William C. Larmore..............39
Fun in America Before Electronics
    by Judy Becker......................44
Black Gold
    by Louise D. Flanders...............50
Beyond Infamy
    by M.L. Anderson...................53
The Escalator
    by June Parks........................60
Surprised by a Dash of Nash
    by Diana J. Baker...................64

A Night at Brighton Beach
       by Toni Kiriakopoulous.............70
Mama Takes a Trip
       by June Parks........................73
The Magical Porch
       by Linda Hayes.......................79
A Slice of Americana
       by Nadine Blyseth...................86
One Nation Under God
       by Beverly J. Powell................91
Memories of Special People and Times
       by Martha Morgan Ureke...........93
Our Musical Heritage
       by Jack Elder........................96
The Place I Belong
       by Mary Bowen.....................103
An American Childhood
       by Diana J. Baker..................109
Leaf Day Remembered
       by Linda Hayes.....................115
The Edge of Innocence
       by Eddie Snipes.....................122
Long March to Fort Sill
       by Marcus Beavers..................128
Through the Eyes of Old Glory
       by Pam I. Barnes....................136
The Flag I Will Never Forget
       by Cheryl Anderson Davis.........141
The Uniform
       by Susan M. Watkins...............146
My God My Country
       by Stephen Caravana...............153

The Ugly Sofa
   by Louise D. Flanders..............157
Our Triumph
   by Eddie Snipes.....................161
American Kaleidoscope
   by James Franklin Gardner........167
Hope for All Seasons
   by Cherise Bopape..................168
The Cabbage Patch Christmas
   by Barbara Holloway...............173
The Magic Pot
   by Lynn Nester......................179
The Day My Daughter Danced
   by G. Lee Welborn..................184
Triumphant Transitions
   by Sue Schultz......................190
America, Home of the Brave
   by Patty Rocco.....................196
A True Southern Gentleman
   by Mary Bowen.....................202
The Best Christmas Ever
   by Judy Parrott.....................207
Where are the Bees?
   by Burl McCosh...................213
Interview with a Seagull
   by Charlene C. Elder..............217
Let Your Light Shine
   by Bonnie Greenwood Grant......220
God's Country - Joe's Resting Place
   by Stacy O'Reilly...................224
Seeds of Hope
   by Lynn B. Pugh...................227

AMERICA'S SYMBOL OF HOPE

America represents the "land of hope." As far back as the early 1600s, people endured severe hardships and death to come to a majestic land of hope and liberty. We live in volatile times and many question the legacy of hope. Some statistics about suicide, financial failure, and crime, for example, illustrate our lack of hope, but information relating to immigration and population growth demonstrates the living promise for a better tomorrow.

Determined to find America's best symbol of hope, I loaded up my turquoise and white VW van and began traveling from coast to coast to find the *one* symbol representing the sense and measure of hope upon which our ancestors founded a new country.

Numerous people from different lifestyles, backgrounds, ages, and communities answered my poll of what "best" symbolized the hope of America. Since the answers and opinions differed, it was up to me to discover what constituted the greatest symbol of hope in America.

My quest started in Washington, D.C. where everyone looks for answers. I stood amazed at the grandeur and magnificence of the marble, limestone, and granite edifices, which house the core of America's democratic government. Hiking up the steps of the Lincoln Memorial, I studied the large sculpture of Abraham Lincoln exemplifying a real symbol of hope for all ethnic backgrounds. Many years ago, he made a stand for freedom, paying for liberty with his life. The hope of freedom is a strong ideal, tough enough to carry a country through extreme tribulations. At the opposite end of the reflecting pool, stands the world's tallest obelisk—the Washington Monument. It is a memorial to the first president of the United States, George Washington, sometimes referred to as the father of our country. The capitol buildings stand as sentinels where our representatives work to preserve our hope through governing laws and regulations. Walking down Pennsylvania Avenue, I peered through the fence surrounding the White House, where the current President of the United States lives. Many American citizens exercise their right to vote and choose who they want to represent America in the world.

Rumbling north in my van, I ventured down Fifth Avenue in New York City gawking at the tallest building—the Empire State Building—a monument to financial hope. Traveling on to the tip of Manhattan Island, the Statue of Liberty came into view, often called the "Beacon of Hope." Did you know France presented the statue to America as a symbol of freedom and hope? With the torch of enlightenment, Lady Liberty loomed as a welcome sight for immigrants heading for Ellis Island and their induction to America, the land of hope.

My next adventure required that the old van drive north to Plymouth, Massachusetts to the docking place of *Mayflower II, a* replica of the original *Mayflower*. Surprised by the small size of the vessel, I learned how each person received only a tiny allotment of space for travel. No matter how difficult the trip, the people persevered because their desire to live in a land of hope outweighed the suffering, which represented a sacrifice worth taking even to the point of death. The awareness I gained from the experience so moved me that I couldn't speak as I walked back to my van.

My schedule included several lighthouses on the East Coast and I wondered if they might be the symbol of hope in America. Their steady light guided many sea captains as they sailed through stormy seas looking for a ray of hope.

One of the original symbols of Christian hope is the anchor, which holds the boat steady in the worst of storms. Yes, the anchor is a symbol to consider, although most people never see one.

My next appointment incorporated Philadelphia, Pennsylvania where the address on the brochure pointed to Market and Sixth. There I saw the Liberty Bell, a weighty, but flawed, symbol of America, tipping the scales at 2,080 pounds. Many times the bell rang out, announcing the hope of liberty. However, this cracked American symbol no longer rings for freedom.

In South Bend, Indiana, I admired the main entrance of the University of Notre Dame. Maybe hope resides in the excellent academic system of America. My van broke a clutch cable when entering, so my search slowed down a bit. I took this as a sign that more than my clutch was broken and removed the great universities from my list.

Early in our nation's infancy, the bald eagle became the symbol of strength and freedom. Though not bald, the eagle's image appears on the great seal of the United States and on many official government articles, including US currency. The mighty eagle soars high above the turmoil of life on earth, yet civilization creeps into its environment and crowds out the eagle's quest for greatness. This majestic symbol of America is on the endangered wildlife list. Will the old bird survive as a national symbol?

Contemplating other animals to symbolize hope, I remembered the bison that roamed the vast plains before man almost eradicated them. In times past, our country's nickel honored the image of the buffalo. My high school mascot—the grizzly bear—represents a symbol of power, but not hope. Many unique and magnificent creatures roam the American landscape, but none great enough to stand as the symbol of hope.

There are many great iconic symbols of America. I admired the awe-inspiring Grand Canyon. Its multi-hued beauty held me breathless. Carved by the hand of God, the huge canyon amazed me with its glorious splendor in an otherwise barren desert.

In my further travels, I discovered many powerful images. Mt. Rushmore in South Dakota features magnificent carvings of former United States presidents. Carved upon the rocky face of

Stone Mountain, Georgia is an impressive scene of three figures in the Confederate States of America.

I held the railing tightly next to the powerful flow of water rushing over Niagara Falls and listened to its deafening roar. My trip included the Grand Tetons, Rocky Mountains, Yellowstone Park, Yosemite Park, Smoky Mountain National Park, the Petrified Forest, and many other natural wonders. Nevertheless, as magnificent as each are, I couldn't label any as the one symbol I sought.

Along the rocky West Coast, I drove the length of Highway 101 from California to Oregon, witnessing the beauty hidden within the harshness of rugged creation. Mighty redwoods thrived for hundreds of years. One giant redwood had an opening in the base the size of a car. They could be symbols, but man cuts them down—in minutes changing the landscape of hope.

Near the 210 freeway in Duarte, California, stands the great hospital complex called "The City of Hope." Many enter through their doors with high hopes that the expert doctors and staff will provide physical healing. Across America, medical facilities and institutions offer a measure of hope as they perform intense research to eradicate some of the debilitating and life-threatening diseases so prevalent today. I thought of the children's hospitals who dedicate all their resources to provide hope for life, and a future.

While in San Diego, California, I saw the largest American flag and learned that it weighs 3,000 pounds (more than the bronze Liberty Bell). It takes 500 people to hoist the giant flag up the flagpole or hold it open on a football field.

The American flag has taken several forms in its evolution—representing America for her honor, liberty, and justice and surviving two world wars and countless other conflicts. Displayed at every government building and many private locations, the red, white, and blue is the most recognized symbol of America. For many who answered my initial poll, the flag was the choice for best symbol of America.

Driving past schoolyards and parks where children played, I pondered how children are the hope for our future as tomorrow's leaders, parents, and workforce. Each individual child will make his or her mark, for good or bad. We hope and pray for their good choices.

Through my exhaustive, but stimulating search for what is the most significant symbol of hope, I crossed the length and breadth of the United States of America. In my observations, one consistent component stood out. Against a brilliant blue sky, or framed by a blaze of autumn-colored hues, a white steeple stands as a lone sentinel pointing to the place where true hope emanates. Our ancestors founded America on religious freedom and faith in God. He is the source of all hope. We find hope where His people gather to worship Him and proclaim the good news. For me, I name the church steeple as the grand symbol of hope in America.

~ Jack Elder

A LASTING LEGACY

It was late November 1676. The harsh fall winds off Cape Cod battered Constance Hopkins Snow's farmhouse. Constance's husband, Nicholas Snow, had died three weeks earlier. After his funeral, the grandchildren stayed to help their grandmother.

Today, Constance felt her age. While her grandchildren were handling the outside chores, she struggled to lift a heavy pot of stew and hang it on the hook over the fire in the hearth. Nicholas had loved her stew. She smiled as she secured the pot and let her thoughts take her back in time. Her family survived the *Mayflower's* treacherous journey across the ocean. She and Nicholas met at church and it was love at first sight. They married two years later.

She smiled at the memory of their wedding day, but felt the sharp pang of her recent loss. Oh, how she missed him. Together they survived many hardships over the years, yet even from their small and difficult beginnings in Plymouth and Middle Plantation, they enjoyed a wonderful family and a rich life in America.

Her thoughts were interrupted when a log from the hearth fell over, sending sparks up the chimney. Constance adjusted the logs. Hearing the children on the porch, she hurried to the front door, slid the sturdy wooden bar away, and yanked the door open.

"Hurry in now, children. This cold wind will only get worse, and you look like you're half frozen. I'm glad you finished the outside chores so fast." She closed and bolted the front door. "Now hang your coats up and get yourself over to the fire."

The children knew better than to balk at their grandmother's instructions. They did as they were told and huddled together, soaking in the warmth from the burning logs.

Rebekah shivered and stomped her cold feet, declaring, "I want it to be summer!"

Her grandmother wrapped another shawl around the youngster. "You will have to wait awhile, Rebekah."

"Aw, Grandmother," Jonathan said, pushing Rebekah out of his space. "Can't Joseph and I stay outside and knock the cones around?"

"No, Jonathan. But all of you may play games inside after we have something warm to drink."

Joseph and Jonathan grabbed the brooms by the fireplace and went to work sweeping the floor while the girls set the table.

Constance poured either steaming hot cider or tea into her special china cups. "Please be careful, children. These cups came all the way from England, you know."

They smiled. All of them knew what their grandmother expected when it came to proper etiquette.

"Grandmother," Elizabeth said, holding the cup and saucer with both hands. "Tell us the story of your trip on the *Mayflower*."

Constance took a sip of her hot drink. "Oh, my goodness," she said. "You've heard that story so many times before."

"Please," they begged in unison.

"All right, then." She took another sip before beginning. "Let me see. It was a long time ago, you know. I was just a child. The ship was bigger than anything I'd seen before and I remember feeling frightened. I didn't know what it would be like going to a new country. I was sad to leave my friends and other family members because we had already moved twice, once after my mother died, and then again after my father remarried."

"What did Grandfather think about the trip?" Joseph asked.

"I didn't know your Grandfather Snow then. Remember, I was very young when my family and I came to the new land. If I'm correct, he came to America several years later on another ship called the *Anne*."

Jonathan set his cup and saucer on the table. "May we move the chairs and table around and pretend we're on the *Mayflower*?"

Constance nodded in agreement. "Finish your cider and tea first. Then you may play."

Jonathan and Joseph guzzled their cider while Elizabeth, Rebekah, and Rachel sipped their tea like dignified ladies. When everyone finished, the table was cleared. As the children moved furniture out of the way, Constance located some multi-colored braided mats similar to the ones she had sat on during the voyage.

"Here are some mats you may use," she said, handing them to Joseph. "Place them side by side because that's how it was on the *Mayflower*."

The children settled down, taking their places. "Grandmother, Joseph's arm is poking me in the face!" Elizabeth complained. "Tell him to *move over*."

Joseph poked Elizabeth again.

"Now children, don't you remember I've told you that there wasn't much room on board?"

They quickly settled down.

Constance sat in her rocking chair and continued. "The days were long. My new mother insisted we keep up with our studies. My older brother, Giles, read while my younger sister, Damaris, and I busied ourselves with needlework. The ship rocked back and forth. It went up and down on the turbulent seas."

"You mean like this?" Jonathan asked, demonstrating the rocking motion by rolling into his siblings on both sides.

"Grandmother," the others cried out.

"That's enough, Jonathan."

"What did you eat?" Elizabeth asked.

"We ate whatever they gave us. Sometimes we had eggs and cheese, but it certainly wasn't like eating at home. I really got tired of those hard biscuits and dried meat." Constance made her grandchildren laugh, pretending to chew and swallow the dry food. "At least we had milk to drink.

One amazing experience I'll never forget—when my baby brother, Oceanus, was born. They moved my stepmother to a different area and gave her privacy while several midwives helped. I was very frightened, but my father assured me that everything would be fine."

Rachel's eyes grew big. "Was everything all right?"

"Oh, yes. You remember this story ... your great-grandmother Hopkins let me hold Oceanus the next day. He was so tiny."

Joseph sat up on his mat. "Didn't you have to live on the *Mayflower* over Christmas?"

"Yes, we did; in fact, we had to stay on the ship all winter because there weren't any houses to live in. We were so cold and very uncomfortable. We sang hymns on Christmas, prayed, and ate together, but many people were sick. Unfortunately, quite a few people died before spring. I was sick once, but I recovered and was fine after that."

Elizabeth raised her hand. "Where did you live when your family got off the ship?"

"In huts, just until we could build a real house. Our first house wasn't as nice as this one your grandfather built. You remember what a good carpenter he was, don't you?"

"Yes."

"Your great-grandfather Hopkins served as an assistant to the governor for a short while and your grandfather was Eastham's first town clerk."

"But why did your father and mother come to America?" Rebekah asked.

"They wanted religious freedom. They wanted to worship God as we had in Holland and to live their lives based on the Bible, as we do now. My father also felt there would be more opportunity in America compared to the struggles in Holland and England."

Elizabeth jumped up and rushed over to hug her grandmother. "Oh, Grandmother, I don't want you to die like Grandfather did."

Constance held her granddaughter close as tears clouded her eyes. "I want to be here a long time, too, so I can see all of you grow up and make me and your grandfather proud. God has given us a wonderful place to live that holds numerous opportunities. Always remember to love God and follow Him. I pray that you'll be able to do great things in America, and perhaps someday you'll be famous. Then you will have your own stories to tell and pass on."

The rest of the children abandoned their mats and gathered around their grandmother, each one touching her shoulder, arm, or hand. She smiled at them. "Don't ever forget that each of you will always have a special place in my heart."

Constance Hopkins Snow died the following year. Following her example of fortitude and faith, Constance's grandchildren went on to help build this country, and her life is still remembered in America, the land of the free and the home of the brave.

~ Charlene C. Elder

WAVE UPON WAVE THEY CAME

From the east, west, north, and south they came.
A motley group of immigrants
None could blame
Fleeing persecution, famine, and war.
On they came.

Coming in waves guided by an unseen hand,
Millions in search of opportunity.
At first by sea, and then by land
Looking for a better life.
On, on they came.

Shuttled through Ellis Island
To be questioned, tested, and documented
Before being cast on a foreign land
To fend for themselves.
Coming, coming, on they came to America.

In search of roots,
At the mercy of the unknown,
Knocking, knocking to find a route
To prosperity
Coming in search of what they knew not.

Gathering with like-minded
In ethnic enclaves
Struggling to see, though often blinded
By the sweat, blood, and despair.
On, on they came.

Struggling to rise above
The masses to make their mark.
Longing, wishing to fly as a dove
Beyond the squalor of the tenement.
On, on they came.

Listening, watching for a chance
To escape the throes of hopelessness.
Looking for that olive branch
Extended to the more fortunate.
On they came.

Learning English,
Studying the Constitution,
To test and accomplish
Citizenship.
Coming, coming of age.

Finding their place,
Making their mark.
With little regard for race
Melding Americans,
On, on they came.

A handful in Colonial times,
Swelling to millions,
Raising children to climb
Beyond the dreams of their ancestors.
On they came.

Forming, molding a nation.
Breaking through ceilings.
Opening up a station
Never known in the old country.
On, on they came fulfilling the mandate:

"Give me your tired, your poor, your huddled masses yearning to breathe free, the wretched refuse of your teeming shore. Send these, the homeless, tempest-tossed to me; I lift my lamp beside the golden door!" —*Emma*

~ Nadine Blyseth

FREEDOM AND OPPORTUNITIES RING

The early morning mist hung heavy in the air, shrouding her silhouette against the pre-dawn sky. She'd been waiting tirelessly for them that September day, and finally after months of careful coordination, they were about to meet for the first time. The family had elaborately prepared the children for her introduction and their excitement mounted as the time drew closer. Just a few minutes more and they'd finally be in her presence, making all the sacrifices worthwhile.

My grandparents and great-uncle awakened the children from restless sleep to end one dream and begin another. Rousing themselves, they quickly dressed and clamored on deck still rubbing the night from their eyes. It was a momentous occasion. As the babes struggled to open their eyes, the elders dabbed tears away from theirs. Clutching the ship's cold handrail, they leaned forward to further close the gap between the lady and themselves.

Rising out of the clouds with her orchestra of seagulls and ocean waves, Lady Liberty beckoned her heartfelt welcome into New York's harbor. As the travelers moved slowly past her resolute form, they were speechless—removing their hats in respect of her willing gift. Prayers of gratitude went up to God who held this country in the palm of His hand after our founding fathers requested His sovereign leadership on Virginian shores in 1607. Fellow shipmates audibly sighed at the sight of their new home. They were each bringing their dreams to be planted in this fertile soil, whose trees were reputed to grow money. Leaving all they had ever known behind was a difficult price to pay in exchange for a gift they could never repay. This new land unselfishly offered in great abundance what other lands couldn't—*freedom*. With an unwearied arm thrust into the air and a glowing torch scratching the sky, the Statue of Liberty safely guided them into the bounty of America.

    In the excitement to reach the ship's deck and a coveted spot at the rail, my two-year-old uncle grasped his greatest treasure, a china teapot. Not sure where he was headed, he took his solitary item of highest importance and scampered toward the early morning light. In anticipation of seeing his new home and the resulting pitch of the ship with all souls lined along one side of the vessel; a tragedy occurred for the youngster. The perfectly seated lid of his beloved teapot was coaxed by gravity and lost its footing, plunging into the dark depths of the harbor. It would prove to be the last thing taken from him before coming into his new country that more than amply returned his earliest sacrifices.

Ellis Island was the first soil to greet their weary feet. Processing an average of 10,000 immigrants daily, the lines were long and colorful with a variety of languages spoken. First was two weeks quarantine on the other side of the property, at accommodations prepared for this purpose. Undaunted by their cramped surroundings, my family focused instead on the dream America promised, and set about establishing their new temporary home.

America was very different from the life they left behind. As European nobility and master linguists fluent in eleven languages, their sacrifice was substantial. Elaborate homes and servants to care for their needs were forever a thing of the past. Days would no longer be filled with riding horses and hunting, or traversing vast amounts of owned land. There would be no more diplomatic dinners, balls, operas, or official engagements. No more couture, commissioned jewelry, or personal art collections. No brandy and cigars. Everything they knew previously was left behind. Time captured permanent change with the Bolshevik uprising and first-hand accounts of their tightening grip. Opposed to their brutal tactics and following their personally escaped kidnapping, my family knew their influence could no longer help either themselves or others; their old world would never return. It was gone forever, as the new order forced itself upon the people. Though not wanting to leave their beloved country, they realized decisions were being made *for* them, and the freedoms of America now ignited their hearts.

Following a highly coordinated travel route spanning several countries (which included disguises on horseback and their two small children concealed in baskets on the horse that carried my grandmother posing as a Cossack); they eventually reached the shores that would carry them to freedom. As was customary, all treasures were secretly buried on the estate. Their remaining monies were spent on those who secured their safe travel to the ship, and upon arrival in their new country, they had a combined $37 to start a fresh life in a foreign land.

Subsequent generations can hardly appreciate the risk and tenacity of their early family's resolve without the beneficial aid of recollection. It seems impossible that anyone would leave the comforts and privileges of a former life to come to a land and life of stark uncertainty. Yet myriads did this when America opened her arms to the tired, poor masses yearning to breathe free. Millions of Americans have similar stories of grandparents and great-grandparents leaving their homeland for freedom's shore.

Precious little was packed for their journey to freedom. All family heirlooms, treasures, and symbols of nobility were left behind at the family estate. Only the most practical items secured passage with these travelers. Each was allowed one personal item due to extreme space restrictions. My grandfather chose to bring our official family crest on rolled parchment authenticating our sealed nobility. It was carried at great personal risk, for if it had been discovered, death was certain. My grandmother brought sentimental items from her father. Artistically gifted, my great-grandfather's exceptional talents were highly demanded in Eastern Europe. It is my lifelong dream to travel back to the old country and attempt location of his public works gracing the ceilings of cavernous cathedrals, depicting religious icons and biblical scenes. As a wedding present to his daughter, he designed and crafted earrings with a matching necklace possessing several precious stones set in solid gold. My grandmother hid this gift aboard ship, but inadvertently fell asleep one night during the two-week ocean crossing wearing the pierced earrings. She awoke after one was torn from her earlobe. Left wounded and missing an earring, the remaining jewels were brought to America.

Upon release from Ellis Island, my family headed west to claim their new freedom. They disappeared into the melting pot of a metropolis to start their new lives. While they were multi-lingual, their training as master linguists was of little use in the new world; English was not one of their spoken languages. It would be an arduous ascent, with all equally starting at the bottom. But America offered an invitation other countries could not. If you possessed drive and determination, there was no limit set for your accomplishments. Long hours were clocked working in steel mills or scrubbing marble floors on hands and knees, but eventually enough money was earned to start a family business. America gave them the opportunity to begin anew, and they seized it.

The entire family became citizens. But my own mother thrust a new stake in the ground and was the *first* to be born on American soil, something she proudly pointed out when older. Mom held this in the *highest* patriotic regard and viewed it as a kiss on the forehead from America itself.

Despite the ensuing Great Depression, the new Americans banded together and helped their neighbors in any manner possible. Food and services were bartered. My grandparents' table, in their second-floor flat above a bakery, often hosted many families who would have otherwise gone hungry. Regardless of their noble upbringing, they were genuine people with the same needs as everyone else, and it was impossible to guess their background given their sincere love for fellow Americans. *This* is the backbone of our country, those hard-working, dedicated immigrants who weren't afraid to break a sweat, reach for the moon, and catch it!

I am a proud American. Proud of what America offered to struggling immigrants without regard to origin. I allow my tears to spill freely when my country's flag is unfurled and flaps for freedom. I enjoy these hard-won freedoms and the resulting safety they bring. This country has given me a powerful Christian heritage and I value that God is solidly at the helm of our government.

I owe a debt of gratitude to this nation under God, for it opened its arms and heart to my ancestors and granted freedom and opportunity to a duke and duchess that embraced this country as their new sovereign. They willingly left the old behind and adopted the new, accepting all its protocol. My grandfather never flaunted his previous station and position in life; his manners were impeccable when introduced to a woman. Grandpa still clicked his heels in unison while bending forward to kiss her extended hand. I believe he would have done this to our Lady Liberty as well.

~ Susan M. Watkins

THE LETTER

The squeal of the wagon wheel urged me on. *Hurry*, I told myself. I could just see the top of my uncle's city hat, a bowler, as it bobbed over the tall meadow brush. My aunt laughed at something he said. Dashing through the cornfield, I ignored the dried stalks that whipped at my face. As I ran into the yard, I heard Pa hammering new shoes on our old mare and Ma whistling while savory aromas wafted through the open kitchen window.

My uncle helped his pretty wife down from the wagon, swirling her in the air as they shared a private laugh. I watched from a respectable distance, not wanting to interrupt the magic moment. I was only two years old when they married, too young to remember. Now I was sixteen and quite curious about such things. They had no children, but I understood without being told that they had something special. Before they married, my uncle lived in what we called the "Wild West." I loved to hear his stories. Now they lived in Cleveland, a good six-hour ride from here, so I knew they must be hungry, but secretly hoped for a story before dinner.

"Howdy, Uncle Ed," I called to him after he had settled his wife inside. He was about to take the wagon and horses to the barn.

"Darrin, my boy. You sure have grown," he said. I jumped onto the wagon with my uncle as we headed to the barn. Unlike Pa, Edward was a businessman. Of average height, he had well-trimmed graying brown hair and an elaborate mustache, which tilted as he gave me one of his easy smiles.

"Edward, it's good to see you. Where did you get the new team?" Pa called out in greeting as he came out of the barn. His laughing eyes showed his pleasure.

"I won them at an auction," said Edward, his brother-in-law.

"You do well at auctions, don't you?" asked Pa.

"What other auctions have you won, Uncle Ed?" I asked, grabbing a bag of oats.

"Quite a few years ago, I won an auction that changed my life."

"Tell us about it," I said, and happily plopped down onto a bale of hay. I was going to get my wish.

"I was too young for the Gold Rush of '49 in California," he began. "Men raced to the West to seek their fortune. Few of them returned, and fewer still made any fortune. Those hills and fields pull on a man, and sometimes he can't let go …." He was in a reflective mood, and spoke to no one in particular. Then he seemed to snap back to the present and looked at us.

"When the early settlers of Colorado discovered gold in '59, Denver City grew up out of the dust over night. By the time I arrived, it had become the business and social center for prospectors all over the Northwest. Like the cities of California ten years before, Denver had bar rooms, gambling dens, and other sordid entrapments. It was very common to see a man lose a week's worth of earnings in one evening," he said, shaking his head.

"It was hard country, where a miner might leave the settlement and never be heard from again. Undelivered mail would pile up in the city post office, and in early spring, the carriers would auction off the dead mail. Dirt-covered miners would crowd around, hoping to win the thickest letter." He chuckled at the memory.

"One warm afternoon, the auctioneer's ramblings drew me to watch the sale. The bidding was winding down so many miners were leaving. The auctioneer held up a cream-colored envelope, addressed with a delicate, female-looking handwriting. The envelope intrigued me, so I raised the bid to two dollars. My heart pounded as I anticipated a challenge. I was surprised when I won. Outwardly, I acted indifferent, pocketed the letter, and rushed to open it in the privacy of my room.

I pushed aside the twenty-dollar bill that fell from the folded pages, and hungrily read the letter. Until that moment, I had been a contented bachelor, but now I envied the man who should have received this letter. Here, read it."

I opened the yellowed envelope he still carried that was addressed to James Stevens.

My dear James,   June 10, 1860

Your letter from Denver City reached me yesterday. When I think of the great risks you are taking in that wild, unsettled country, I pray to God that you come safely through.

I remember our walks on Sunday to church, where you told me you loved me and your heart spoke from your eyes with a look I cannot forget.

Please come home. The trees in the orchard are bursting with fruit.

Your last letter said that your horse died; please use this money to come home. Give up the thought of growing rich for me, my dearest James; the gamble of your life would never allow me to enjoy it.

I am always your own,

Annie

As I handed the letter back to my uncle, I noticed how his eyes sparkled. *Was it tears that I saw?*

"I joined a large group of miners who headed south that spring, but my mind was no longer on finding gold. The prairie had bloomed with lively colors and sweet fragrances after the spring rains. I leaned back in my saddle and drank in the priceless beauty before me."

They *were* tears! And they began to spill onto his cheeks.

"The next afternoon, we met a posse that described a band of five or six desperate men who were attacking small groups of miners. Victims were found tied up and shot; none survived. The '59 Gold Rush was disintegrating.

That night, we camped in an open grove. We took turns keeping watch for any surprise attacks. The land was flat there, and the soil as black as the looming foothills. We ate supper by the glow of an orange sunset. I took the first watch, and hoped we would evade the trouble I sensed was coming. I woke my friend, Charlie, a big burly man from Missouri, when the horses stirred. Charlie moved into the darkness as the rest of us kept guard. A few minutes later, a pistol shot cracked the silence. We waited for Charlie's return. At first light, Charlie came back to the camp and told us he had hit one of them varmints. We followed a blood trail until we came upon the man Charlie presumably shot.

Two hours later, we came upon the posse we'd met the day before. They were examining three bodies, bound and shot dead. They figured the murdering gang attacked the miners about two nights ago.

'That makes sense,' said Charlie, 'since they attacked us last night.'

'Were you able to identify any of them?' the leader asked.

'We left one dead, two hours from here.' Charlie pointed in the direction we had come.

While Charlie and the leader continued to talk, I walked over to the three bodies. They had been tied together and shot at close range. I noticed that one of them had a hunting knife tucked into his belt and inscribed on the wooden handle was the name, James Stevens.

As I leaned in for a closer look, an envelope slipped out of the dead man's pocket. The handwriting was unmistakable—it was from Annie.

I placed the letter and hunting knife on top of James' body as we buried him with his two unfortunate companions. I cried for Annie's loss. I didn't know how I would ever find her.

The Colorado Gold Rush, like the California Gold Rush, had left very few rich. Many of the miners of '59 realized the fever was hogwash and returned home.

Twelve years later, I managed a supply company in Ohio that distributed general wares. A business associate introduced me to a gentleman who was a widower and his unmarried daughter, who kept his household. Her hazel eyes held a melancholy I could not fathom, but I was drawn to her confident demeanor. She was tall, slender, and very graceful in her movements. When she heard that I had lived out West, she peppered me with questions about the prairies and rivers, the new cities that evolved from once backward towns, and especially stories of miners who were reunited with loved ones.

One evening, after I answered many questions, she looked at me and asked, 'In your travels, Mr. Baird, did you ever meet a man named James Stevens?'

'You're Annie?' I asked, surprised.

'What do you mean?' she asked.

'It never occurred to me,' I faltered, 'yet, I always hoped to find you.'

I continued to explain about winning the auctioned letter, then later finding James.

'I knew he had died,' she said at last, 'but I could never be certain.' Her eyes grew moist and faraway. A moment later, she looked at me and touched my arm.

'Thank you for searching for James,' she said."

Uncle Edward had tears in his eyes as he turned to walk out of the barn.

"Uncle Ed, what happened?" I cried.

"What do you mean?" Uncle Edward looked at me.

"What happened to Annie? Whatever became of her?" I asked.

Then Edward and Pa laughed, leaving me bewildered.

Finally, Pa answered, "She's in the house with your Ma. Let's go eat. I'm hungry, son."

~ Patty Rocco

FREEDOM TO BUILD

I can't believe I'd even consider doing this, but it is a good idea, Grace thought as she bit her lip.

Lifting the hem of her ankle length skirt, she eased her slender frame into the straight chair at her desk. The small oil lamp before her threw streaks of light across her simple desk and the spare bedroom furnishings.

Grace Eliza McCallie flicked a bit of lint off the bodice of her dress as she considered the issue from every angle. After listening to her father preach for forty-one years, she agreed with his Scottish Presbyterian views. Decisions required careful thought and prayer.

"Mr. Lamp, you wouldn't consider trying to light the entire world, now would you?" Her slim finger touched the base of the lamp. "You'd know just how much oil you have, and you'd be wise enough to scorn such a suggestion."

She paused, considering how to explain her thoughts. "You see, that's just the issue. I know how much I have." Her stomach protested the suggested scheme with a cramp. She opened the top drawer and pulled out her ledger. After flipping it open, she scanned neat rows of handwritten figures.

"My skimpy savings match my meager salary. Teaching doesn't bring much."

The flame seemed to gesture to her as if to say, "But there is more."

She pursed her thin lips for a moment before they curled into a smile. With a decisive snap, she closed the ledger and put it aside. An icy tremor rose from her abdomen. "Yes, you're right. I do have the house on Oak Street. Rental income adds to my salary. Dad wanted me to have something to fall back on—as a spinster."

The suggested business venture would deplete all her savings. A long, deep sigh emptied her lungs. Her breath made the flame flicker for a second.

"There now, you see, your light wouldn't always burn." She raised her eyebrows. "Lots of things could make it stop. You're just like me—vulnerable. An unmarried lady must be careful."

The huge grandfather clock downstairs chimed the hour and Grace rose. "It's nine. I wonder if Dad is in his study."

She walked out of her room and down the stairs. The door to her father's study stood open, and he sat at his desk. With reading glasses perched on his nose and his gray head bent over his Bible, he was studying by the light of an oil lamp.

"Dad?"

He snatched off his glasses and looked up. A smile spread across his oblong face. "Grace! What can I do for you, dear?"

A glance at the clock made her cringe. "I know it's getting late, but I need some advice."

"Of course!" He pointed toward a ladder-back chair. "Pull up that chair and tell me what's on your mind."

"Eula and Tommy approached me today with an idea." She slid the chair close to his massive desk and sat down. "They believe Chattanooga needs a girls' school. The school here doesn't offer courses that prepare girls for college. They would like to open one that would."

"Wonderful idea!" A spark of joy ignited his deep-set eyes. "I favor educating women."

"Ah, yes!" Fear produced a sharp exhale. "The problem is that we'd need money. They suggested each of us contribute one hundred dollars. Then Eula asked to borrow her hundred from me. So really, I'd be the one risking the most money."

His bushy white eyebrows shot up. "But my dear, this is a worthy project. As a teacher you know the importance of education."

"Yes, but something about funding the school myself makes me uncomfortable." She crossed her arms, hugging them to her chest.

He reached over and patted her knee. "I know how frugal you are, Grace. Look at you. You're very pretty, but your clothing is simple. You don't wear any of those expensive frills women waste money on these days. And your hair—I've seen ladies come to church with big fluffy hairdos. You keep yours fastened into a sensible bun. I'm sure you'd be the best one to manage a tight budget."

"They want to use my house on Oak Street for the school." She licked her lips and rubbed them together several times, a nervous habit she had since childhood. "Right now a family lives there that pays rent. Wouldn't it be better to save the house for extra income?"

He paused a moment. "No, I think you should use the house. The three of you could live upstairs, and use the downstairs for classrooms. When the school gets bigger, you'll need to find a larger building. But until then the house will work well."

"But Dad, do women start businesses?" Her chest tightened and her lungs wouldn't accept all the air she tried to suck in. "This project frightens me. If you recall, several people have started such schools. Each of them failed."

He shook his head and crossed his arms. "Honey, this is 1906. We live in a free country. Yes, a woman can start a business. You know Chattanooga has grown in the past few years. We have a free market and the economy here is good. I think you'll find plenty of parents willing to pay for education. You must offer excellent teaching, but then, you already have the teachers."

"Yes, Eula is my cousin."

He chuckled. "She practically grew up here. Her honesty is unquestioned. And I'm sure her teaching is exceptional. What about Tommy? I don't know her."

"Tommy is a superb teacher. She teaches with me at Chattanooga High School. I've got a great deal of confidence in her."

He picked up his glasses and polished them with his handkerchief. "Now, honey, you'll have trials. That I can guarantee. I believe, however, that learning to lean on God will make you stronger. I know! You were born just after the War Between the States. Since God's grace provided for us throughout the war, I called you Grace. The Lord will sustain you."

"I remember hearing that story."

He smiled and fingered his worn Bible. "We can be thankful that we live in a land where we are free to worship God. What a privilege to teach the next generation of mothers and wives. I believe God will bless you and your school."

"I'm pretty apprehensive." Hot tears leaped to her eyes. "Will you pray with me, Dad?"

"Of course!"

Grace watched as her father slid his bulky frame onto the floor by his desk. With a brave smile, she brushed aside her tears and knelt beside him on the unpolished wooden floor. Reverend McCallie draped his arm around his daughter's thin shoulders and closed his eyes. She listened to his deep voice as he bathed their venture in prayer. With one slow, deep breath she sensed God's grace and peace.

In the fall of 1906, Grace McCallie and her partners Eula Jarnagin, and Tommy Duffy opened the Girls Preparatory School (GPS) in Chattanooga with only a handful of students. In September 2005, hundreds of GPS students and faculty members held a special celebration in downtown Chattanooga to celebrate the beginning of their 100th year.

~ Cynthia L. Simmons

ALOHA

My father, Wendell Carl Greenwood, was a slender 5'11" man with black wavy hair and dark blue eyes. He was the oldest of twelve children and the only one with my grandmother's Scotch Irish coloring. He was so handsome—according to his mother, "I would have to shoo the neighbor girls off the front porch every morning. Girls these days are so forward," she often told people.

In 1929, nine years after my dad's birth, diphtheria swept through America. It claimed my father's seven-year-old brother and later almost forced my grandfather into prison because be refused to have my father vaccinated. When the authorities tried to take my grandfather to court to force him into allow doctors to vaccinate his son, his comments made the newspapers and he became part of the great debate. People strongly lined up on both sides, and it lasted for months. My grandfather argued that Jesus could—and indeed would—heal Wendell and that doctors certainly did not know everything, quick to point out that people were still dying after receiving the vaccination.

After Jesus *did* heal my father, my grandfather became a Pentecostal minister. He worked as the head cashier for the U.S. Postal Service by day and as a pastor in the evenings and on Sundays. My grandparents' activities went from card playing and dancing to praying and singing.

For my father, my grandparents' changed lives meant the end of spending time with his mother shucking peas on the back porch and spending time with his dad in his workshop. When Dad became a teenager, he chaffed at these new and strict rules. His interests had crystallized into two areas—sports and music. He played the Hawaiian guitar, enjoyed sports, and secretly listened to sports and music on the radio.

Concern grew over his rebellious son, and in an effort to unite Wendell with his church family, my grandfather asked him to play a hymn on his guitar for the congregation. Dad practiced until he had the hymn memorized and he felt pretty cocky about his talent. However, on the day of the performance when he looked out at the church pews filled with people, his mind went totally blank.

The tension mounted as the silence grew. Everyone waited for Dad to begin his song. Finally, in desperation, he started playing the only thing that came to his mind—Hawaiian songs. The melodic tone of the Hawaiian guitar filled the church and he started to feel pretty good, until he looked up and saw his father storming down the aisle. He knew he was in for big trouble. His father, thinking Wendell had deliberately tried to embarrass him, was furious.

On the drive home, they shared a serious father and son talk, resulting in a mutual respect for one another. In the days that followed, my dad joined the United States Coast Guard. The incident became a family joke that gets funnier each time it is told.

~ Bonnie Greenwood Grant

THE WAY IT WAS

The giant old stranger looked cold, tired, and hungry. He showed up standing on the milk room porch of our farmhouse, located near Dahlonega, Iowa, on the coldest evening so far of a specially harsh and snowy March. I had never before seen anyone like him!

Myself, I had already joined the Larmore family back in 1917 in the Ottumwa Iowa Hospital—nicknamed "Bill" for William and destined to be an only child. By this particular night in 1930, I had already learned about drought, dust, useless crop replants, and foreclosed farms. Some city relatives were out of work, and I remember waiting with Dad in a failing Ottumwa bank as it swallowed our savings. I also will never forget not even having 10 cents on some Saturdays to go see Tarzan. All such had become poked in a bitter word "depression," which even we kids knew and feared.

Our farm was at least a half-mile from any other home place and five miles from the nearest city, Ottumwa. Yet the railroad that passed through our land on its gleaming, mindless way brought frequent company to our doorstep. Many homeless and hungry men in those Hoover days rode the rails from one town or state to another looking for work, and often moved from one disappointment to the next. In those days, truly lazy men were hard to find. If they were jobless in Des Moines but happened to hear that Morrell Packing Plant in Ottumwa was hiring, they might hop a Rock Island boxcar and ride the rails down here hoping to get on. They didn't dare ride all the way into the Ottumwa rail yards because the rail guards would beat them up and throw them off the freight. So when the locomotive pulling the boxcars slowed almost to a walk while huffing up that steep grade on our land, the free-booters would drop off. Realizing that they were still almost five miles from Ottumwa and Morrell's, they would look around to get their bearings. They could see our buildings in the daytime or our lights at night and would come to us in hope that we might help them on their way. We always did, and the great big old man I am about to tell you of was no exception.

  Dad opened the milk room door and held up the kerosene lamp to see, but did not invite our visitor into the house right away. That had proven to be a bad idea in the past. In one such case, only monster growls from our dog, a big collie named "Laddie," sent one character quickly on his way.

  This time, Dad and our strange visitor had a long man-look at each other. Then they both grinned and Dad asked him into the kerosene lamp lit, coal stove heated, cream separator milk shed. Even stooped as he was, the man banged his head on the door. He topped my dad by at least a foot. I was sort of shook, but Dad, being himself, was in no ways scared. In a fight, my small but fearless dad would probably have bitten him on the knee. However, none of the past railroad drop-offs had been any more peaceful and quiet than this one. He spoke maybe ten words in a husky whisper to explain himself and then kept his mouth shut. Even my warmhearted little mama could find out nothing more about him.

We helped him out of his tattered winter coat, cap, and gloves. Next, we offered him a seat in the big old brown rocking chair and got him thawing out by our potbellied stove. Mama was handing out cups of hot coffee as fast as he could gulp them down, and we could see he was finally getting warmed up. Then Mama gave him a heaping bowl of beef stew we had left from supper and began fixing for his night's stay with us.

We loaded him up with blankets and a couple of thick comforters. Dad and I got my old Eveready flashlight and lit his way out to our warm barn. We spread the blankets over a mass of timothy hay from the east mow and he stretched out. We pulled his boots off and piled the comforters over him.

"There'll be no smokin' in this barn!" said Dad firmly. Our visitor smiled, nodded quietly in agreement, and pulled the top comforter clean over his white head.

The next morning, about five o'clock, only scattered snowflakes were falling and the porch thermometer showed minus three degrees. As Dad and I entered the barn for our morning chores and milking of our eight cows, the big man was still under his covers. We were back in the milk shed with me cranking the De Laval cream separator before he came to the door. He was carrying the neatly folded blankets and comforters.

At Dad's invitation, he came inside and put the bedding on the door bench, and then seated himself at the old pine table by the stove after his whispered, "Good morning."

Mama brought him a breakfast plate of what we would soon enjoy—scrambled eggs, bacon, and fried potatoes. Then she set a hot pot of coffee and a big cup next to his plate. That feast he shoveled in silently and we three watched him as if he were part of the Barnum and Bailey circus. He surely wasn't the ordinary tramp. No way!

With his meal finally down the hatch, he rose to his full great height, groaning softly as his worn joints stretched. Then, without haste, he prepared to leave, dressing himself completely in his old winter clothes, even to the ragged furry cap with earflaps. He turned towards my mama and dad and wordlessly reached his ungloved right hand to Dad, who, of course, accepted it warmly. He did the same with me. Then he turned to Mama, bowed in a courtly old-world manner, and amazed us by his next action.

In a clear voice, *deep and strong*, he spoke these words of Jesus that I had once learned in Sunday school but had forgotten: *"*... INASMUCH AS YE HAVE DONE IT UNTO ONE OF THE LEAST OF THESE, MY BRETHREN, YE HAVE DONE IT UNTO ME."

Smiling quietly down upon me like a leaning mountain peak, the giant waved farewell to us as would a king. He silently left our farm and strode away through the bitter cold down Hill Road towards Ottumwa. We were never to see him again, but he left behind a sense of innate nobility of our land and living that had not been there for us before, and I will never forget him.

~ William C. Larmore

FUN IN AMERICA BEFORE ELECTRONICS

My earliest recollections of electronic devices are of a radio and a telephone. In 1936 when we had our house wired for electricity to replace gaslights, we acquired a medium sized, static-emitting radio with the design of a gothic window over the speaker cloth. Already hanging on the wall when we moved into this house was a rectangular wooden telephone with an adjustable mouthpiece. The receiver hung on one side with the ringer on the other.

What a contrast to today's combination devices as we listen to our favorite songs play on cellular phones, which most of us use today for more things than talking. Allow me to take you back to a time in America when children played in innocence and found joy in simple physical activity, nonsense, creativity, and laughter. In the early '40s, we went to the Saturday cowboy matinee for a dime, and loved to imitate our favorite stars. I was ten years old, and even though a girl, saw no problem with strapping on my holster with the silver six-shooter and imitating Tex Ritter.

We also found great pleasure exploring the creek down in "the holler" in front of our house. We lived on the last street exiting town, which faced another high hill. These narrow valleys are called "hollers" in that part of the country. In the summer, we would catch crawdads, corralling them into a pebble fence as we competed to get the most. We also enjoyed simple treasure hunts, searching for extra heavy wine-red rocks that we called iron ore. They were rare. To find one called for sharp eyes. After every storm, our creek unearthed more treasure. (In later years, when studying geology in college, I learned that our red treasure rocks were actually hematite, a form of iron ore.) In winter, the creek offered other pleasures. Giant, stalactite-sized icicles hung from the huge rocks that formed on a wall set back from the edge of the creek. These inspired us to raid Mom's kitchen for paring knives so we could carve them into diamonds. It was cold work for our frozen hands, and proved fruitless in the end when they melted, but admiring our gems offered great fun while they lasted.

  One particularly cold night, everything froze solid. We discovered a bumpy, slippery slide of ice had formed where a steeply descending rivulet emptying into the main creek had frozen solid— even the tiny waterfalls. We pretended to flee from an imaginary monster while trying to climb it, continually losing our footing. I still remember my little brother rolling over in giggles as we slipped and slid in our frantic attempts of fake desperation. What fun! That creek provided many delightful hours in my childhood. When I was a young mother, I wished for such pleasures for my own boys, but their creeks never seemed to measure up to mine.

We had much more freedom moving around back then. When I was ten, I had horrible buckteeth. My two front teeth stuck out so far that I could not shut my mouth. My parents, although quite poor, took me to the big city to get them straightened. I began the ordeal of having braces and monthly visits to my orthodontist. I had to travel alone for two hours on a Greyhound bus to our capital city, Charleston, West Virginia, walk from the bus station to the orthodontist's office, and then after my appointment I would catch a city bus and go across the river to spend the night with my Aunt Vi who lived in South Charleston. In the morning I would retrace my steps, taking the buses back to a Greyhound bus stop located fifteen miles from my home. I waited there to be picked up by my parents, but one time they seemed to have forgotten. I had no money to use the public phone, so I walked five miles to a friend's house, and her mother called my parents. As I look back today on this time of my youth, I think of the dangers that I was spared and shudder.

Then we moved to my most favorite place while I was growing up. My father was a Methodist minister, so we moved every two to three years. In time, we lived all over that state. During World War II, we moved from the center of the state to the southern tip, located in the Appalachian Mountains. While we were there, the "war to end all wars" ended. Optimism filled the air and America rejoiced in the peace. Sugar rationing ended and we had bananas and sweet treats because the Nazi subs no longer blocked the shipments to Cuba.

We lived close to my dad's father. At age eighty-six, he had slowed down considerably and we visited often to help with harvests and provide wood. He and Aunt Sally, my step-grandmother and his sixth wife, lived in an isolated valley hemmed in on three sides by mountains. They had no electricity or gas, so they cooked and heated their home with wood. Today when I smell hickory smoke, I vividly recall Aunt Sally's kitchen.

As a teenager, I helped my dad cut down a dead hickory tree with a crosscut saw. Then we secured it with a chain attached to our harnessed horse and snaked it out between the trees. I rode atop Grandpa's horse, Dolly, back to the house. It was great fun! Once there, we cut the log into sections that Grandpa could later split into kindling for the cook stove. I can visualize that woodshed now, next to the walkway to the kitchen that was paved with smoothly worn river stones.

I remember one time at Grandpa's farm when several of the family had gathered. All my cousins and I played games of hide and seek, and tag in the barn. To avoid capture, two of us jumped from the hayloft and landed knee deep in the large manure pile along the back of the barn. It was a soft, mucky landing, and since we were barefoot, we were not injured. Besides, the springhouse and water trough for the horses was only thirty feet away. As we cleaned up, we laughed uproariously at our daring escape. This may not have necessarily been *clean* fun, but it was fun nonetheless.

We were highly influenced by the 4-H club, and fortunate that the state 4-H campground was located in our county. Most 4-H clubs were in rural areas and taught young people necessary skills about farm life. The 4-H recreation leaders taught us locals the Southern Singing Games featured at the state camp. They were so much fun that we included them in all our social functions. Even at our high school dances, we played Skip to My Lou, Four in a Boat, and Bingo. I particularly loved to play the dance version of Bingo. As in all the games, everyone sang the words as we played. It went like this:

The farmer's black dog sat on the back porch and Bingo was his name, Oh.
The farmer's black dog sat on the back porch and Bingo was his name, Oh.
B-I-ngo, B-I-ngo,
The farmer's black dog sat on the back porch and Bingo was his name.
B – I – N – G – Oooo.

     As the game began, alternating boys and girls held hands in a big circle and marched around the gym, singing lustily. But after the third round of "The farmer's black dog sat on the back porch," everyone stopped. Each girl turned left and took the right hand of the boy behind her in the circle. Then they loudly called out the letters of the dog's name, spelling B-I-N-G-O as the girls alternated hands with the boys, and repeated this until they stopped at "O" This boy picked up the girl and swung her high, completely around. Then we all grasped hands once more as the game repeated itself. As we spelled out the dog's name, the girls began anticipating who would be the next boy for letter "O." If he was large or muscular, you could anticipate a big swing. The boys competed in this swinging, each trying to outdo the other. We laughed and laughed; it was so much fun. We also danced to the popular tunes of our times as music played on hard wax records, and liked the slow dances when the lights were turned low. Our favorite regular dance was the polka. We alternated regular dances with the Southern Singing Games, which we played in the bright light.

How different it is today, with music 99% beat and 1% melodic noise. Dancers face one another and jerk various parts of their body to the beat. I wonder, *how can this be fun*?

Today's fun seems to be mostly a spectator activity. Young children sit glued to the TV set. Boys and girls, even adults, are addicted to computer war games. Watching football instead of playing it has become a sport. Would our world be a better, gentler place without modern technology especially that which purports to entertain us electronically? I wonder if America's youth today has as much fun as we did when we used our imagination and creativity so freely.

~ Judy Becker

BLACK GOLD

Every year on Veteran's Day as communities and churches honor the men and women who served our country, a wave of regret clouds my memories. Many people who never served in the military valiantly served our country, yet they received little or no recognition. My dad was one of those heroes.

For nearly half his life, M. J. "Bubba" Davis mined black gold in the oil fields of Louisiana, Texas, and Mississippi. Daddy began his career with Texaco Oil Company soon after graduating from high school in 1939, just prior to the outbreak of World War II.

His brother-in-law worked for Texaco and managed to get him a job working on the offshore rigs in the Gulf of Mexico, on some of the original American oil rigs many miles off the Louisiana coast. "I was too young to be given much responsibility and had to start out doing kitchen duty in the commissary. Eventually, they moved me into the production end and I got to work on the rig itself," Daddy recalled.

He often remarked that getting used to life on an offshore rig was one of the toughest adjustments he ever had to make. When he first went to work on the rig, the sound of the huge motors kept him awake at night; however, he overcame that obstacle quickly when his supervisor put him in charge of the noisy motors. He became so accustomed to the racket he would suddenly wake up during the night if they stopped working for some reason.

In 1941, the United States entered World War II, thrusting the oil industry into high gear. People employed in this industry were all but excluded from the military draft because the nation's oil supply was so critical to the war effort.

Daddy told us that their work was sometimes dangerous. On several occasions, German submarines targeted the oilrigs and supply ships in the Gulf of Mexico. I remember the stories Daddy would tell us, "One time, the Germans sank three ships in one night. We strung up blue lights to provide lighting to work by at night. The Germans couldn't see the blue lights and it kept us hidden from their submarines."

According to Daddy, submarine raids were frequent in the Gulf of Mexico. "A liberty ship was brought in that had taken a hit above the water line," Daddy dredged up from memory. "The hole in the side of that ship was big enough to drive a Cadillac through, but since it was above the water line, it didn't sink."

Not all the ships were as fortunate. On one occasion, the German U-boats hit their mark, a heavily laden fuel barge. It was loaded with 100-octane aviation gasoline used to power the fighter planes. Daddy said that the fire from that gigantic explosion lit up the sky for miles.

Daddy survived his "military" service during this war era in the Gulf of Mexico and continued his career with Texaco in Texas and Mississippi. He retired with over forty years of service, but his heart never left the oil fields.

Though he never served in our nation's Army, Navy, Marines, Air Force, or Coast Guard, whenever I'm asked if my dad served in the military during World War II, I am always tempted to respond with a very proud, "Yes."

~ Louise D. Flanders

BEYOND INFAMY

It was a dreary, December Sunday morning. Sleet tapped on the windows, while inside our cozy home in Munster, Indiana were the familiar aromas of coffee brewing, burnt toast from my little sister's cooking quests, and stale starch from my mother's endless ironing. The big radio played softly in the background as our warm radiators popped and hissed. There was no church today; the roads were too bad. A cold, lazy day lay ahead, and only 18 more until Christmas.

Papa was in the living room, just starting to read the heavy Sunday issue of *The Chicago Tribune*. With Christmas fast approaching, it seemed every department store, especially Goldblatt's, stuffed the newspaper with extra advertisements and sale fliers. Of course, I knew I couldn't even think about touching the paper until my father was finished. So I sat on the floor, still dressed in my flannel pajamas, and passed the time by working on a project for my social studies class. I was 14, comfortable in my childhood, and not too anxious to grow up. And Christmas was coming.

I liked to clip articles about the war escalating in Europe, to try to support my novice views on isolationism. Mama would say I was idealistic. "Son, it's not a perfect world we live in, and we may someday have to help our friends over there," she coached. It seemed like many of our neighbors agreed with her.

The "one-world" concept was foreign to my way of thinking. I only wanted to have fun, and war was not my idea of that. The only bad guys I cared about were the cowboys dressed in black on the big screen down at the Alvin Theatre.

Once Papa finished with the paper, I leafed through, but there didn't seem to be many articles that interested me. I had extra time to read my favorite section—the "funnies." My mother was still ironing and my sister, Barbara, was now trying to cook cream of wheat.

The radio program, that no one appeared to be listening to, was suddenly silenced. The unfamiliar pause caused us to halt our activities and we glanced around the room at each other. Then a stern-voiced announcer came across the airwaves and said, "Stand by for an important announcement from the President of the United States." Again, a pause, and the sound of silence prompted our family to remain motionless. It was as if the whole earth stood still. I wondered, *What is going on?*

Mixed with static came the burdened voice of our president through the radio speakers. He told us that Japanese military airplanes had launched a surprise attack on the Pearl Harbor naval base. They bombed many of our ships and buildings. He called it "a day that will live in infamy." At that moment—no one knew why—time was frozen.

When the president was finished talking, I could hear myself swallow hard as I remembered to breathe again. The radio then returned to its regular programming. My father spoke first. "Those dirty Japs!" he said with disgust. The seed of anger towards this apparent adversary began to grow. What was happening? Are the planes coming here? Will they bomb Munster? I was impressed by the seriousness of my parent's conversation, but lacked the wisdom to know what it all meant.

None of my family members knew exactly where Pearl Harbor was located. Mom thought it was in Guam. I guessed it was in the Pacific Ocean, near the Philippines. My father said it was a territory of the United States, like Wake Island, but wasn't sure where. Barbara got the globe from the bookcase. We found Pearl Harbor located on one of the Hawaiian Islands and began to fear for the people who lived there. My mother said we should pray. What was I to pray for? Where was God? Was He sleeping in this Sunday morning?

The war raging in Europe had been going on for some time now. The steel mill my father worked in sold scrap iron to Britain, which was used to make combat airplanes. In school, we were told of Adolf Hitler, and we perceived him as a bad person who must be stopped. It seemed the Italians were assisting the Nazi war effort—and now the Japanese too.

Europe always seemed so far away. It was the other side of the planet, as far as I was concerned. We were living comfortably in America, with a big ocean on either side of us. Why did God let this happen? Why now? It was almost Christmas. I didn't want to think about war.

Papa turned off the radio, and headed out to his workshop where he went when he wanted to be alone. As the day went on, his frustration lingered. My father was a proud American. He always seemed disappointed that he was born too late to fight in World War I. Now Papa would be too old to serve in our armed forces. My mother decided she and my sister should make gingerbread—right then. I think she was protecting little Barb from worrying about the tragedy we just heard of.

I got dressed. Bundled up in my bulky winter garb, I climbed through the snowdrifts, finally arriving at my best friend's house. Harvey and I spent the afternoon wondering about our future, when we would be old enough to enlist in the Army, and if our girlfriends would miss us when we did. As we listened to his parents' conversation, we heard their angry words towards the Japanese, "Well, that's it. We're surely going to war now."

Later that night, after the rest of my family had gone to bed, I tuned in to the news broadcasts on our radio. Reports were now trickling in about the casualties from Pearl Harbor located in Honolulu, Hawaii. I was saddened by how many human lives were lost. Those families were surely grieving beyond description. As I pressed my ear against the radio speaker, tears welled up in my eyes. I softly prayed, "Please God, help me to understand what's going on."

The following day at school, the talk was tough amongst fellow students. Anger reigned supreme, and was directed at the Japanese. Even my social studies teacher seemed filled with hate as she remarked, "We need to pay them back for what they did to us."

I telephoned my friend, Evelyn, after dinner that night. She attended Catholic school so I was certain she knew more about God than I did. I asked many questions. Did she know what God was up to? Would it be better by Christmas? We talked for an hour. She was the only one who felt some compassion for the people of Japan, but then Evelyn always did look for the best in people.

I only knew one Asian family. They operated a laundry on the north side of town near Lake Michigan. Their oldest daughter, Suzy, was in my homeroom. She didn't come to class that Monday after the bombing and I never saw her again. I'm not sure if she was Japanese, Korean, or American. People were angry at anyone who had "slant eyes." Ironically, many of my friends had a German heritage and no one seemed to liken them to the Nazi aggressors. Maybe it was different, somehow, because no one from the war in Europe had actually touched us like this bombing at Pearl Harbor. How would God straighten all this out?

Spontaneously, the consensus was that the United States would join the war, and very soon. The isolationists became silent. Those who disliked President Roosevelt now supported him. The world was changing fast, and I was changing with it. God was beginning an important work in me.

The following Sunday our church pews were packed. There were many people I had never seen before. The church furnace was on the blink again, and everyone stayed bundled up in their coats. It seemed the entire congregation was searching to find God's direction and encouragement.

I listened to the choir singing Christmas carols like never before. With every word of every verse, I was changing. No longer was I a selfish, shallow-minded, small town teenager living only for the fun in each day. I believe I was standing on the threshold of conscious maturity, becoming a spiritual man of God. In this time of certain war, I began a new journey and put aside my childish thoughts and ways.

In the weeks to come, the United States *did* enter the war. At first, no one thought it would last too long, and then came reality with rationing of gasoline and rubber. I missed the Sunday afternoon car rides our family could no longer take. World War II labored on for four more years.

The United States and our military allies were eventually victorious. Soldiers came home. Families were reunited. American life as we knew it returned.

The events of that Sunday in December will live forever in my memory as a benchmark of my youth. I was forced to grow up, like it or not. It was a season of conflict and contrast. While our nation was preparing to go to war, I was surrendering to God and allowing Him to direct my steps.

For some, December 7, 1941 was "a day that will live in infamy." By definition, infamy refers to *wickedness, evil,* and *disgrace.* But for me, this day was much more about the love of family, honor of country, promise of life eternal, and God's wonderful gift of redeeming grace.

~ M.L. Anderson

THE ESCALATOR

My steps faltered as I stumbled onto the escalator that was moving slowly upward. I hoped I would not tumble back down the moving steps. I leaned against my friend's shoulder, mostly for reassurance. I was struggling to be an "upstanding citizen" and not fall down. This feat to maintain my dignity was bringing back a distant, traumatic memory.

On Saturdays, when my sister, Betty, and I were little girls, Mom would drive us from our hometown in Griffin, Georgia to the city of Atlanta for a day of shopping. We would go to Rich's and Davison-Paxon's each weekend and ride the nine cent "shopper's trolley" between the two pre-mall competitors.

In Griffin, one of our main upscale stores was Crouch's. They sold clothing, bedding, and home furnishings. Because I was a kid, each sales lady seemed ancient with gray or salt and pepper-hair. Each was required to wear black or navy and most wore fussy, crepe dresses. They looked like they were going to church. Their shoes were very sensible and square-heeled. To me, all the women looked alike.

These sales clerks didn't seem to compete with each other for customers, but they were always glad to assist Mom because she was a regular shopper who usually made several purchases. One sales lady would be chosen each Saturday to operate the ancient, noisy elevator so there would be no sales commission for her that day.

In Atlanta at the Rich's store, uniformed men staffed the elevators. The operator would announce, "Watch your step, please" upon your entrance to the lift in his deep, manly voice. Then he would continue, "Second floor, women's fashions, shoes, and children's wear," as we headed up.

At the second floor, the people who were waiting to get on the elevator would be asked to "Step aside, please." The riders would exit and the waiters would enter, turn around, and stare mindlessly at the fancy metal scrollwork doors until they opened to release them from their cage.

Then the elevator operator would say, "Third floor, furniture, curtains, linens, and gift wrap. Over to your right and down the aisle is the famous Magnolia Room." Even though we ate lunch in the Magnolia Room almost every Saturday, I don't think I ever ordered anything but my favorite—a scoop of delicious chicken salad on a crisp lettuce leaf, served with their unforgettable frozen fruit salad. Their famous recipe is now served in the Swan House at the Atlanta History Center in Buckhead, Georgia. A wonderful little fruity muffin was on the side and, of course, southern sweet tea.

One particular Saturday in 1942, we came upon a new phenomenon in Rich's. They had installed an *escalator*. When I researched this, I thought Rich's had outdone Davison's, but found out that Davison's had installed one in 1927. However, nobody would use it, so it was removed.

My mom was scared to ride the escalator. The clanking, moving steps looked terrifying to her. But she was assured that we could still ride the old elevator, which we did. She wanted to protect her two girls like a good mother hen over her chicks.

Another time, as our shopping spree at Rich's was about to end, Mom steeled herself and bravely walked toward the feared escalator. Many "floor walkers" (Mom's name for the bosses) in their sharp, navy blue suits and fancy ties, were milling around, smiling broadly to the customers.

For some reason, Mom decided we would try the escalator. I hesitated, but was the first one to step on. I grabbed the handrail to steady myself as the giant metal steps immediately moved me toward the lower level. It was scary. At the top, Mom kept holding Betty's hand, even though Betty had slowly stepped on and was following me down. Mom froze and could not bring herself to step on, but she also would not let go of Betty's hand. The only words she could speak were "Whoa! Whoa! WHOA!" getting louder and more frightened with every inch Betty descended. All of the bosses were alerted and ran to the escalator. Betty's eyes looked frightened and I started to cry. What was I going to do without my mother at the bottom of this contraption?

After some confusion, someone suddenly turned a key in the gleaming metal slot located at the top of the stairs and the escalator came to a sudden, jolting halt. Everyone that was riding it grabbed the handrail to keep from tumbling domino-style to the bottom. One lady simply sat down to keep from falling.

Only then did Mom let go of Betty's outstretched arm. Everyone stared and Mom gave the people a wan smile. We recovered and with wobbly legs *walked* down the escalator.

I remember this experience so vividly because it was so traumatic in a little girl's eyes, but it is only one adventure from my exciting, eventful life. I can assure you this one will never be forgotten. And to this day, when I ride an escalator, it brings back this memory that is now so funny.

~ June Parks

SURPRISED BY A DASH OF NASH

The human mind is one of God's most awesome creations. Like a computer, it constantly receives data and meticulously files it into compartments for future use. Often, a seemingly insignificant thought passes through my mind and sets off an unexpected chain of memory reactions.

One day, I was shopping and noticed a brand of toothpaste that I had used as a child but had not purchased as an adult. Unable to resist the urge, I bought a tube "for old times' sake." The following morning as I brushed my teeth with that toothpaste, I was shocked to hear running through my mind—with full orchestration—the tune of that product's TV jingle that I had heard in the 1950s on the first TV set my family had ever owned. Yes, the human brain is one awesome computer!

As I searched through my amazing computer brain for ideas of what to write about in this collection of memories of America, I found some interesting information stored there. I've always loved reading and writing poetry, especially the humorous kind. I often write God-inspired poems filled with deep spiritual insights, but there are times when I write in *granola bar style*—a mix that includes fruit, nuts, and flakes.

    I pondered when I had developed such love for wacky poetry, and I recalled English class during my junior high days. We were required to memorize and recite a certain number of lines of poetry each week. About that time, on a shelf in my parents' bookcase I discovered a fascinating poetry book filled with the poems of Ogden Nash, and I immediately fell in love with Nash's humor. I was especially fond of his crazy four-liners, which I often quoted in English class when the poems I had memorized fell short of that week's requirements.

    Poems still alive in my memory bank like:

A girl whose face
Is covered with paint
Has more chance with me
Than one whose ain't.

and

I think that I shall never see
A billboard lovely as a tree.
Indeed, unless the billboards fall,
I'll never see a tree at all.

    Judging from the laughter and comments of my fellow classmates, they loved Nash's poetry as much as I did, and either my teacher was a Nash fan herself or she simply enjoyed the break from the usual poetry routine.

I decided to search my bookshelf as I pondered these things, and there it was—my old, dilapidated copy of the third edition of *The Ogden Nash Pocket Book* published in February 1944. Excited, I sat down and began to read and reminisce.

On the first page I read, "*IMPORTANT— This is an original POCKET BOOK.*"

Wow! I thought. *This book was one of the earliest paperbacks ever published!* As I turned the page, I saw a picture of a hand dropping a single scrap of paper to the ground. The heading read, "It's only a Piece of Paper." That page encouraged Americans to save and collect every available bit of paper to be recycled for use in the war effort. It explained that when used together, scraps of paper could be made into valuable items such as containers for blood plasma for our soldiers; airborne containers for dropping food or medicines to liberated people; helmet linings, gun covers, ration containers; or even shell cases and bomb bands for the bullets or bombs that would help stop the war. The page ended with this plea: "Save every scrap and you'll help end the scrap!"

After reading a number of my favorite poems on tattered pages still marked with dog-eared corners, I finally turned to the last page. There I was surprised to read, "*OUR BOYS NEED AND DESERVE BOOKS.*" Readers were encouraged to cooperate with "The Victory Book Campaign" by sending used paperbacks to American soldiers. It urged those who had finished reading the book to take it to the nearest library or post office and have it mailed for the amazing price of a 3-cent stamp to the Army or Navy library at one of the addresses given.

On the back cover of the book, within a small stamp-sized square, it was stated, "Send this book to a boy in the armed forces anywhere in the US." It was then that it hit me ... the book had probably been mailed to my own dad (now deceased) when he was serving our country in the Navy during World War II!

My eyes filled with tears as I sat pondering my discovery. I thought about my dad and other American heroes—the thousands of soldiers who had fought valiantly during World War II and other wars to secure the freedoms I now enjoy. I was reminded of the sacrifices our soldiers and others are making today as we are engaged in war in Iraq and Afghanistan ... soldiers who are far from home and family ... their husbands or wives who are raising their children alone ... their children who are growing up without a mom or dad around to hug them, play with them, read to them, and enjoy the milestones in their lives ... their parents and grandparents who are separated from their soldier children and grandchildren ... their friends and neighbors who miss their company ... and their employers who hold jobs for them until they return.

As I thought about all these things, I realized how much I took my freedoms for granted. I asked the Lord for forgiveness and thanked Him for freedom and the other blessings He had bestowed upon me. I then renewed my commitment to diligently pray for our troops and vowed to find more ways to bless our military men and women and their families.

I'm sure if Ogden Nash were still alive, he would be surprised to know his small book of poetry is still inspiring Americans to reach out to American troops. I realized just how powerful written words are, not just at the time of their writing, but for a lifetime.

My hope is that Ogden Nash's words have tickled your funny bone and lightened your day, and that his words and mine have inspired you to pray for our troops and reach out to them—perhaps to even send them books like others who sent books to my dad and his fellow soldiers during World War II.

I also hope you were inspired to search your memory banks for those hidden surprises that you can turn into powerful written stories to touch and change people's lives. Whether you write humorous poetry like Ogden Nash, dramatic fiction adventures, or life-changing nonfiction, send your words forth to make a difference. Who knows, you just might become famous!

I'm glad I was surprised by an unexpected dash of Nash, and I'm grateful for forerunners like him who "turned over my tickle box" and taught me the value of laughing at life and its crazy idiosyncrasies. I am thankful that they inspired me to use my freedom of speech and writing skills to inspire and entertain others.

Now in closing, I leave you with a brief quote from Nash's poem, "Don't Grin or You'll Have to Bear It":

People who have senses of humor
Have a very good time.
But they never accomplish anything of note,
Either despicable or sublime,
Because how can anybody
Accomplish anything immortal
When they realize they look pretty funny doing it
And have to stop to chortle?

~ Diana J. Baker

A NIGHT AT BRIGHTON BEACH

On July 4, 1945, when I was a little more than five-years-old, I remember my yiayia (Greek grandmother) saying the war would soon be over and her son, my Uncle Billy, would come home.

Yiayia helped Bill, her sister's son, who owned two restaurants and a couple of concession stands along Brighton Beach in Brooklyn, New York. Her job included making the best clam chowder I ever tasted, but also peeling potatoes to make French fries, washing dishes, and scrubbing floors. My yiayia never complained, and when I look back on those days, I realize what a servant heart she had. She was a praying woman and I believe her prayers had an important impact on me.

One night, Yiayia said, "Tonight we are going to watch the fireworks."

"But Yiayia, we always watch the fireworks on Tuesday."

"Yes, but tonight is special."

After she finished her work, she gave me a Nathans hot dog, a paper cup filled with French fries, and my favorite drink—a Yoo-hoo. After I finished eating, my yiayia and I went to the boardwalk and found a bench overlooking the beach. When my mother arrived, she sat next to Yiayia and held me on her lap.

The fireworks were magnificent that night, and I was in awe of the displays in the sky. The last one was a combination of many fireworks at once that created an image of the American flag—glorious! I thought I heard someone crying. Standing next to us was an older woman, about Yiayia's age. She was clutching an American flag close to her heart.

"America! America! Thank you God for bringing me here. Thank you for this country and for this flag," she said. As I think about it today, I recall her strong foreign accent.

I remember turning to my mom and asking, "Why is she crying and kissing the flag?" My mom told me she was from another country and that she was glad to be in America, where she was free from the bad people in her country. My mom got up from her seat and went to the woman. She hugged her and spoke encouraging words, assuring her that she would be okay.

The woman looked up at my mom through her tears and said, "God should bless you and your family always." I clearly remember those words. (God has given me a great memory, and I can remember many things from the past.) That woman truly understood the significance of the American flag.

Often, we Americans take our nation's flag for granted. Yes, we are patriotic on holidays or in times of war and conflict. During these times, we stand united and display the flag at our homes and even on our cars. But many forget when things are going right.

Whenever I pass a flag, I feel proud that I am an American and that I live in a land where I am free. The 13 stripes on the flag stand for the original colonies and represent unity. They also remind me of the stripes Jesus bore for us—stripes which stand for the eternal unity between Jesus and those of us who love and obey Him.

America has a freedom that no other country has. Christians in this nation share the knowledge of the love of Christ with others who can receive this gift for all people, in America and around the world.

Whenever you sing our National Anthem, "The Star Spangled Banner," think about the line, "gave proof through the night that our flag was still there." Let us always honor our flag and our freedom, and let us pray for God to take back this mighty nation, which He founded for His glory.

~ Toni Kiriakopoulous

MAMA TAKES A TRIP

Mama dreamed up the whole thing, and then talked her enthusiastic buddy, Miss Nettie, into going along with it. Two mamas, each with two kids, planned to invade Miss Nettie's relatives in Maryland for a week.

Her sister's farm was beautiful with sprawling acreage out in the country. Their two-story farmhouse looked like a postcard from the Georgia countryside with familiar rambling porches and grassy lawn, yet they lived only an hour's drive from our nation's capital. It would be quite a trip from our small town, Griffin, in middle Georgia to Maryland.

Being from the South, and because we were respectful, my sister, Betty, and I addressed our mama's friend as Miss Nettie, who I will always remember as a bundle of energy, doing everything in a hurry. She had big eyes, set on a round face framed by medium brown hair softly sprinkled with gray. She was curvaceous and always dressed in fancy flower-patterned dresses.

This was a very fashionable era. Everyone wore hats: men, women, and children. It was during World War II. The men wore fedoras like those that you see in old pictures. The women's hats fit close to the head with few embellishments. Things were simple in those days; there were not many extras. Every weekend we dressed up and went shopping, or strolled around downtown with Miss Nettie's family, and ended every Sunday afternoon with an ice cream cone.

Mama and Miss Nettie were cloth inspectors at a cotton mill that made beautiful, high quality sheets. The work was demanding and the bosses were tough. The two women were good friends. On workdays, they could not talk over the noise of the loud, clanking machines. The bosses frowned on their gabbing—they were there to *work*!

As the trip north was planned, Mama decided that our two families would tour Washington, D.C. There were six of us: Mama, my sister, Betty, and me, Miss Nettie and her two kids, Annette and Eddie. Poor Eddie was outnumbered and he wouldn't have a completely happy day the whole adventure.

We got tickets to take the Greyhound bus to Maryland to visit Miss Nettie's sister on her beautiful farm. That was the only mode of transportation we could afford. Besides, the driver knew the route better and it would be safer and cheaper than driving our own car.

Our clothes were already packed neatly into suitcases. However, Mama insisted we take extra hats in a large hatbox. That meant suitcases, handbags and that huge hatbox to lug the whole trip.

The big day finally came—August 14, 1945. We were preparing to leave when there was a huge explosion of people pouring into the downtown streets. It was V.J. Day, which marked the end of World War II! People rejoiced as they danced in the streets. Everyone was ecstatic.

Our departure was supposed to be in the middle of the day, but there seemed a sudden shortage of buses. It was nearly dark when our bus finally came. We really didn't want to leave this local celebration; for years, we had waited for this day. Everyone had sacrificed and learned to live with only the bare necessities and we wanted to be with our friends and loved ones at such a momentous time. What a glorious day!

The time came to board our bus. As people pushed and shoved, our mamas kept a close eye on us; counting heads to be sure we were all still together. Suddenly, as if on cue, the string holding the hatbox broke, and hats of all colors and sizes scattered everywhere. We dove under the bus to retrieve several that rolled away. Mama stuck a hat on everyone, including Eddie, and almost put one on a stranger. Eddie had the urge—but not the nerve—to object. There wasn't a thing he could do but wear his fetching hat onto the bus.

The big motor coach slowly worked its way through the crowded streets. We hung out the windows, cheering and waving. All along the 40-mile route to Atlanta, people waved and yelled, jumping up and down. There were fireworks going off everywhere. It was a wonderful, long-anticipated day.

When our bus finally arrived in Atlanta, the driver could not find a parking place at the station. He could barely snake his way through the celebrating crowds. As we changed buses, we had to be watchful that all our bags and family members got on together.

Then there was the long, arduous trip to Maryland. Somewhere around Kentucky or Virginia, we had to change buses again. All available buses were probably needed for transporting the troops because the last leg of our journey was in a school bus. I had never ridden in a school bus, or experienced that bouncy, bumpy ride before. I walked across the street to my elementary school, and walked the four blocks to high school—uphill both ways.

Once we finally arrived in Maryland, we learned that our hosts had to work almost every day, so to tour our capital we had to arise before dawn and ride in the back of Miss Nettie's brother-in-law's truck. We nearly froze as we traveled in the early morning mist. The traffic going into the city was terrible, and by the time we climbed out of that truck, we were ready to rest, not tour. Nothing was open at that time of the morning, so we had to sit outside until exhibits, and government buildings opened their doors to tourists. I could have used that time to sleep in.

I was a teenager, the oldest of the kids. Mama had just started letting me wear lipstick and high heels. I had new shoes for the trip; they were brown with a decorative bow. They weren't the spiked heels I wanted, but sensible ones with squared, two-inch heels—the highest Mama would allow. I loved those shoes and will never forget them.

One day we toured through the Smithsonian Museum. I had begged to wear my new shoes. Mama questioned it, but she allowed me to wear my adorable brown shoes. Soon, my feet swelled and hurt so bad I could think of nothing but sitting down. When our ride came back for us that afternoon, I felt such relief as I hung my swollen feet off the back of the truck, letting the air cool them. But I kept my precious shoes on, afraid that if I took them off I might never be able to get them back on my feet again.

At the Smithsonian, I loved the displays of our presidential first ladies' fashions and elegant tableware. Lindberg's plane, that made history with its flight across the ocean, was hung from a ceiling in a huge room. It looked so small and unimposing; I could not believe it accomplished that outstanding journey. The U.S. Mint, the Lincoln Memorial, and our nation's capital building impressed us as well.

On Sunday, at the farmhouse of Miss Nettie's relatives, all the kids rode horses and played to our hearts' content in the shady yard. I ran barefoot in the thick, cool grass and we swung on a big tire swing that hung from a giant oak tree. We knew our amazing vacation was about to end, so we savored every quickly passing minute.

Retuning home, we realized our country had just experienced a powerful time as we finally came to the end of World War II.

Many unforgettable memories came from that trip, and Mama made her great dream for her girls and her friends come true.

~ June Parks

THE MAGICAL PORCH

The year was 1950 and America was preparing for war again. Daddy put on his uniform and left every weekend. He told me he was building up his airtime. When I asked why Daddy couldn't play with me any more, Mommy said he had to learn to fly all the new planes. One Sunday evening he burst in the door gesturing to the shiny bars on his hat. Mommy gave him a really long kiss and then left the room with tears in her eyes. Picking me up so I could play "airplane," he announced he was now a captain in the Air Force Reserves.

Since Daddy worked for an airline, we got passes to fly to my grandparents' house every summer. This year, my cousins were already in Augusta because their daddy had been deployed. I didn't like that word because it meant daddies left home and kids had to move in with their grandparents. Some of my classmates left school because their dads were "shipped out."

When we arrived at the airport, I discovered Daddy wasn't going with us. He always flew with us! Instead of checking his big B-4 bag with ours at the ticket counter, he carried it into his office. He sat in his wonderful, swivel desk chair and pulled me into his lap. Holding me close, he explained that he was leaving on another flight to go to soldier camp for a while. He wasn't being deployed; he just had to go learn how to be a better pilot. We'd have the whole summer to play with our cousins and he'd see us soon.

When we arrived in Augusta and pulled into the driveway on West Avenue, a surprise awaited us. My cousins, Sandra and Sheryl, burst through a new side door cut into the single car garage. They dragged us inside to show off their new home. Needing to secure a place for his family while he was away, my uncle had built a couple of miniscule bedrooms and a bathroom. A kitchen now occupied the place that had once been Granddaddy's workbench.

There were several other changes. Inside the main house, the big front bedroom was now rented out to a lady who worked at the bomb plant. Ruth was her name. She was nice and we only had to be quiet at night. Best of all, since our daddies weren't there, we each had our own bed instead of pallets on the floor!

Being kids, relocations, and survival on a soldier's dole didn't trouble us. These were pre-television days before the advent of home air-conditioning. Moms shooed kids outside after breakfast, and readmitted them for lunch and naps. We drank water out of the garden hose and had to ring my grandmother Mur's funny doorbell for permission to pass through the locked screen door for our potty breaks. Our mothers provided this quality playtime so our imaginations would properly develop.

My grandparents' little stucco house was special. Its unimposing front porch was magical. The only visible adornments were a glider and two metal rocking chairs. Two large square pillars rose above small concrete platforms that flanked wide steps. One abutted from the house about twelve inches. That small gap was the portal into a vast realm of infinite adventures.

Sandra matched me in age, and Sheryl always teamed up with my sister Diane. The porch provided a secluded place of refuge from the scorching summer sun. Mur kept a stash of dress up clothes for us in a box behind the glider. Once kisses and hugs were duly dispensed, we headed straight to the porch to stake a claim on the terra cotta tile floor. Nine squares made up our private domicile where personal props and treasures were secure. The rest of the space was public domain.

Sandra and I particularly enjoyed being princesses. Our role models were the English royals. Princess Elizabeth's wedding seemed straight out of our storybooks. The porch became a beautiful castle. We would emerge from our dressing room as lovely ladies with long flowing hair. A bobby pin securing an old scarf completed the illusion. Worn housedresses and clomping high heels that had seen better days soon became ball gowns and glass slippers.

To enter the castle gates we had to go down the top step, take another step over to the concrete wall, and then slip around the thick pillar balancing on a narrow, two-inch ledge. The danger of negotiating the treacherous pathway lent a bit of spice to our make-believe play. Prickly holly bushes became our moat and provided incentive to tread with care.

We would emerge from our magical niche into the great hall that housed our ornate thrones. Seated on the metal rockers, we would arrange our skirts *just so* and prepare to admit our admirers or the local peasantry. While our guests were imaginary, princesses needed a real entourage. Sometimes my cousin and I would be able to bribe our younger siblings into playing the role of groveling yeomen. A couple pieces of candy from Granddaddy's store would usually do the trick.

With a few discards from the cupboards, we created a kitchen where servants would prepare banquet meals. Magnolia leaves became golden plates heaped with berries and sand from the sidewalk. Little Golden Books morphed into gilded platters, which were carried aloft with one hand, fancy-waiter style. Most of the time our dinner would make it to the grand dining table, an overturned cardboard box. Sandra and I would drink from walnut shell cups with little fingers daintily held high—because princesses always dined with stylish grace.

Every once in a while, the serfs would revolt and we were forced to create new roles for them. We allowed them to be ladies-in-waiting, a very important position in the castle. They could wear high heel shoes, don exotic gowns, and have long flowing hair; however, their long hair was a tea towel. Only princesses had scarves for silky hair. Sheryl and Diane were content because they enjoyed the clacking sound of their heels as they went about their various duties. As attending ladies, they could drink pretend tea with pinkies extended.

If the supporting cast wandered off to play on the swing set, make-believe characters stepped into vital roles. In a flash, Sandra and I could conjure up dashing young men, tall of stature with raven hair and winning smiles. Our suitors always had ermine trimmed cloaks and jaunty hats with one curling ostrich plume. Like our beloved Lilibet, we were accomplished equestrians. Visiting princes accompanied us on swift steeds as we galloped through the land. Being elegant ladies of gentle birth, we rode sidesaddle on the arms of the glider. We traveled about the countryside waving queen style to our loyal subjects, who loved us and reverently bowed as we rode past. Because we were polite princesses, we gave them regal nods to let them know we appreciated their adoration.

Life was good in our kingdom. At night by the glow from the entry light, we'd host balls where the most eligible princes across the land came to seek our hand in marriage. Slipping through the portal, we would meet our heart's desire in the formal gardens. Hand in hand, we strolled among the camellias, flowering shrubs, and magnolias. In the center of the yard, a dogwood with low gnarled branches formed benches where lovers could steal a kiss or two.

The *brrrng* of the old twist doorbell would strike the midnight hour signaling the end of our trysts. With a frantic flurry of skirts, we would rush back through the portal into the castle. Quickly, we would fling gowns and slippers into the dressing room of our bedchambers. Reclining on our high canopy beds, we would recount the night's romantic adventures.

The next day we'd climb aboard the royal coach driven by a team of snow white horses. The two metal rocking chairs were maneuvered to face each other and produced a nice rolling gait as we journeyed to visit friends in a far away land. Inevitably, we'd be set upon by marauding bandits attempting to steal our jewels and spirit us away to the castle of an evil ogre. Not being sissy princesses, we always had pistols tucked into our belts. We fought alongside our retinue of outriders as the bullets ran out and our faithful men lay slain. Loud cries for help would usually entice our siblings back into the game with the promise of a rousing battle. Fallen branches were quickly fashioned into gleaming swords. "*To shay, to shay,*" we'd cry as we struggled to force the villains to the edge of the cliffs. With swords swinging and skirts hiked high, we shouted, "*On guard* you curds, give up or die."

We'd seen swashbuckling movies and knew just how to parry and thrust. Holding left arm curled overhead, we gracefully draped our hand and set our feet in the proper fencing stance. Swords flashed as we forced the foe to the edge of the drainage ditch running along the road. Bravely united in purpose, with one thrusting motion, we would send them all to oblivion. Victory was ours!

While we enjoyed the fantasy battles of another time and place, our dads were committed to a real fight. The sacrifices to keep our land free were made by everyone in America. The age of chivalry wasn't the stuff of fairy tales and movie screens. It was enacted by real men and women at home and abroad, who believed in God, country, and the American way.

Because genuine heroes gave their all, we were able to enter the magic portal of a make-believe land were everyone lived happily ever after.

~ Linda Hayes

A SLICE OF AMERICANA

During the early 1950s when the grain had turned from green to gold, I thought the wheat lands of Montana were the most natural place to be. Every possible moment, I was in the fields feeling the wind blow through my hair as I swayed with the rustling stalks of grain. Hoping to catch glimpses of a combine moving across the prairie, I surveyed the vast horizon.

Each July, about the time of the state fair, I asked my dad, "Is it time?" He would break off a handful of wheat, chew the kernels into a little ball, and cock his head. The darkening late afternoon storm clouds told me that Dad was more anxious than I to get the grain into the bin, lest a hailstorm reduce a bumper yield to less than the price of the seed. On the other hand, the elevator would dock us if the moisture content was too high. Dad taught me that we must not cut too soon.

On more than one occasion, he shook his head. "Not yet."

"Can I help?" I impatiently asked.

Dad, my hero, responded, "I can hire help; my daughters don't need to do farm work." However, he had no trouble calling me whenever my small fingers would fit into places his large ones would not. While waiting for the grain to ripen sufficiently, I was his "gopher" as he worked in the shed or the yard.

The day always came when he asked, "Doodlebug, want to take a ride?"

After he helped me climb up to the seat of the big red Massey Ferguson, he started the combine and we bumped and bounced our way to a nearby field. With levers moving in and out, up and down, we cut a swatch to fill the hopper with a bushel or two of grain.

Then, with motor still idling, he scooped up a handful of kernels from the hopper, chewed them into a little ball, cocked his head and …

I eagerly waited … listening … to hear:

"Yes, we'll begin harvest in the morning!"

Mom and I were up before dawn preparing a farmer's breakfast of cooked cereal, eggs, pancakes, waffles, and piping hot coffee for Dad and the motley crew he had assembled to help bring in the crop.

Harvest time meant helping my mother prepare lunches and snacks, and I often got to drive them out to the workers. I could only reach the gas pedal by standing on the floorboard. Imagine a little blonde-headed girl of eight chugging along in compound low in a one-ton pickup, up and down rolling hills for a mile or two until she could catch up with the combines, trucks, and hungry men. That was me—too young to drive by town standards, but never too young to do what had to be done.

While the men ate, I ran through the brittle stubble left in the wake of the combines and caught grasshoppers. I popped a few in a jar, added some fan weed or cheat grass, and watched the pesky critters struggle to escape their glass prison. I'm sure a twenty-first century animal protection agency would have a fit to know—please don't tell—that I liked to dismember my share of the flying insects, placing the legs in one pile and the bodies in another.

"Why not," I reasoned, after hearing about hordes of grasshoppers that wiped out crops during the difficult 1930s Dust Bowl. Besides, what else was there to entertain a farm girl too busy to go swimming with friends during the summer recess from school?

It was work and more work, summer after summer until I graduated from high school and moved away. Little did I realize the nail-biting times my parents must have lived through just to put food on our table and provide for other necessities while they endured conditions beyond their control.

During those growing up years, I never wondered why my family came to Montana—much less America. It never occurred to me to delve into my genealogy. I had a wonderful grandmother who loved to shower me with gifts and she made every holiday special until she passed away when I was only fifteen.

That I was Norwegian didn't seem important; we were Americans—except when my sisters and I ate lefsa and krum kaka and parroted words that sounded like, "tousand tak," which meant "thank you for the food."

After I became an adult, I learned that my paternal grandfather—at the age of sixteen—left his parents, brothers, and Norway to pass through Ellis Island. He moved to Wisconsin where he milked cows on a dairy farm seven days a week, morning and evening. While he did this work for several years, he knew this was not where he wanted to settle down, nor did he want to be a dairy farmer.

He wanted to till his own soil. But he learned not all Norwegian immigrants had the same dream when his friend, Ole Evinrude, approached him with a business proposition. "Thomas," he said, "If you put in $50, and I put in $50, we can build boats."

Rejecting the idea, my grandfather replied, "Only little boys play with boats."

I don't know whether this conversation occurred before or after the Enlarged Homestead Act of 1909; however, by 1910 my grandfather, smitten with land fever, was on his way to Montana to file an application, agree to improve the land, and register a deed of title to 320 acres. His *own* 320 acres!

To my knowledge Thomas and Ole parted ways never to reconnect. One would grow wheat for a nation of immigrants, the other would establish the Wisconsin-based Evinrude Company and manufacture boats and boat motors for immigrants who had advanced beyond the subsistence level.

In 1911, Thomas Selstad married my grandmother, who was a neighbor and Norwegian immigrant. The couple had six children who survived to adulthood during the Great Depression as the family successfully worked the original farmstead. My father was the second oldest son. He carried on the farming tradition by owning his own land near Great Falls, the farm where I grew up.

As a third generation immigrant, I cannot imagine what my paternal grandparents and other pioneers endured braving the harsh winters, droughts, insect infestations, low wheat prices associated with early nineteenth-century farming, all without the benefit of electricity and motorized vehicles. Their memories live on in many ways. A grand celebration was held in July 2009, when Dutton, Montana, commemorated its centennial.

Though I cannot go back to my childhood days, each summer I envision the undulating tapestry of yesteryears—the ripening grain, the grasshoppers, the combines ... and I am once again a little girl celebrating harvest time in Montana.

~ Nadine Blyseth

ONE NATION UNDER GOD

At the start of the school day, a voice would boom through the loud speaker. It was our principal, who led us through our daily disciplines. Included were announcements, a scripture reading, and always the Pledge of Allegiance.

We would all stand together and place our hands over our hearts. In unison, we then recited the pledge. I liked this comforting morning ritual. Each day we would listen for the intercom and pay attention, then stand and repeat our pledge. If you didn't know the words, you would learn.

I feel a sense of pride, as I think back to those elementary days, glad that we took this time each day to honor God and country. For my generation, this customary procedure continued through our high school years.

Through my research, I learned that Francis Bellamy, a Baptist minister, wrote the original Pledge of Allegiance in 1892. President Franklin D. Roosevelt added the hand over the heart gesture during his term, and then in 1954, President Dwight D. Eisenhower added the words "under God."

I pledge allegiance to the flag

of the United States of America,

and to the republic for which it stands:

One nation, under God,

indivisible,

with liberty and justice for all.

I don't remember anyone disagreeing or protesting this wonderful way to start the day. I believe patriotism and faith in God go together. Many died so I could live in a free country, and our military men and women stand silently as they salute our flag.

God's Word instructs us to pass our faith down to our children, and our children's children. Jesus died so I could be free to live with Him. Could it be our responsibility to pass our heritage of freedom to them also? I intend to, and have no shame in expressing it.

Thank God, we still live in the land of the free and the home of the brave. I'm glad to be included, how about you?

God bless America!

~ Beverly J. Powell

MEMORIES ...

Sometimes I like to simply relax and think of nothing in particular. I let memories of my life float around like leaves blowing in the wind. I remember very little of my childhood, but writing poetry is a way I can express the "memory" words I've kept inside for a long time.

Life is made of memories
If we allow time for reveries;
To sit and gaze out a clear window
And see the sun or the water glow,
Or to watch a squirrel scurry through the grass
Looking for buried nuts from summer last;
Seeing how flowers bend in the breeze
Silently bowing, completely at ease;
The trees stand tall, their branches high,
They salute the skies as the clouds pass by.
The waves hit the shore with a thunderous roar
As seagulls gently glide and soar
All these bring back memories of a childhood spent,
Of innocence in life ... that long ago ... went.

There were times set aside throughout the years
When Grandma would rock away my fears.

Grandmas are special, as special can be,
For without Grandma there wouldn't be me!
Grandma is a gift of God's great love
He made her as gentle as a turtledove.
She spoils me a little, but she loves me a lot.
She's been this way since I was a tot.
I love my grandma with a love that's profound
Even when she glances my way with a frown.
Yes, my grandma is special, as special as can be,
For without my grandma there wouldn't be me!

She seemed to know when my fears went away
For it was off to school I went one day.

Teachers are a very special breed,
Earnestly striving to help students succeed.
Always ready to help when asked
Caring enough to seek the best from each task.
Hating to see young minds not being used,
Exploring new ways to keep students enthused
Rarely, if ever, do they receive any praise
Seeking only to keep their students amazed.

Teachers helped me to turn my times of woes
Into times of beauty ... like an American rose.

I am a thorn between all the roses;
But it's not as bad as one supposes.
I stick here all day surrounded by beauty,
I guard the roses because it's my duty.
I keep all away with a prick like a pin,
For I don't want my roses to fall into sin.
I watch each one from a small bud grow
Into the loveliness only God can know.
Each one blossoms in a different way,
Growing more beautiful every day.

~ Martha Morgan Ureke

OUR MUSICAL HERITAGE

America is in love with music. A multibillion-dollar industry records and distributes all things musical. Variety remains endless from Broadway musicals, concerts, and local performances, and from the piano bars to full orchestras with choirs in mega churches across the nation, while America sings, hums, and whistles along. Music is an important part of our culture affecting each inhabitant of this country's population—309 million strong.

My love affair with everything melodious began at birth. Earliest recollections open with my dad singing. Each week, he rehearsed at home preparing for his next Sunday morning solo at church. He selected the great hymns like "How Great Thou Art." You could hear his powerful baritone voice above everyone in the church congregation. His loud voice often embarrassed me then, but I wish I could hear his booming voice again today.

Like most kids who attended Sunday school, I sang the children's songs of the day including "Jesus Loves Me." I remember singing a solo on the radio in a church program at six-years-old. I sang

"Just a Closer Walk with Thee." However, I didn't follow my dad's role as a church soloist.

When my family was on vacation or a weekend visit to relatives, Dad carried his favorite songbooks in "low voice," arranged for bass and baritone singers. Church leaders often asked Dad to sing in the services we visited.

I am happy I was there to accompany my dad when he sang his last church solo. I helped him as the Alzheimer's disease began to steal his mind. He still possessed a great, strong voice. In heaven, Dad sings in God's celestial choir, "Glory to God in the Highest."

My teenage years celebrated a great time for music and my musical repertoire expanded from hymns to rock and roll. My 1951 Ford came equipped with a radio—a real necessity. I picked up my date, tuned in the local music station, cranked up the volume as loud as the law allowed, and cruised down Main Street singing, "Do wah diddy diddy dum diddy do."

We stopped at a diner and sat in a booth with a Seeburg Wall-o-Matic jukebox extension at the end of the table. Sipping a cherry phosphate, we selected our favorites. Dropping my quarter in, I pushed "A5," to hear Tennessee Ernie Ford sing, "16 tons … another day older and deeper in debt."

I listened to the Frankie's, Elvis, and all the "do wop" singers. I allowed all genres of music a generous share of my time and interest. As an older listener, I enjoy a wide variety of musical venues from the classics to the rhythms of banjo in bluegrass.

America functions on music. TV commercials need background music. Producers carefully chose the sounds to stimulate the emotions that complement the sale of their product. Music stirs emotions, opening the mind and heart to both good and bad.

Restaurants, shopping malls, grocery stores, service stations, banks, and most public businesses play songs. They want customers to relax and loosen up, creating a buying mood.

Music is more than a national pastime; it reaches into the soul and spirit, resonating with something in us and calling us to action. Soldiers once rose to the chords of "Reveille" and fell asleep to "Day is Done."

I recall our church organist playing "Tenderly Calling" at the end of a sermon and watching people walk to the front of the church to accept Jesus as the way of salvation and the start of new reborn Christian life. I, too, went to the front to begin my new life.

My eyes mist anytime the flag goes by in a July 4 parade or I hear a marching band play "Stars and Stripes Forever." I get shivers when I hear "Amazing Grace" played on bagpipes and goose bumps when I hear the "Hallelujah Chorus" of Handel's *Messiah*. I close my eyes and drift into the heavenly realm for an imagined sneak peek at God's glorious music.

I graduated from high school to the sound of "Pomp and Circumstance." I married to the sound of the "Bridal March." They will bury me as the organist plays "Nearer, My God, to Thee." All this amazing diversity of sound starts with only seven notes.

America has a rich history of music. Immigrants to America brought their music styles and interpretations. There are genres too numerous to categorize like jazz, blues, country, pop, and gospel. Music fits class, race, religion, language, and gender.

We listen to music alone and in crowds. Large congregations sing together as one voice praising and thanking God for His goodness and love. Hymns, spirituals, and gospel music formed the music of faith. I grew up grabbing the hymnal from the rack mounted on the back of the church pew in front of me, turning to page 267 and singing the first, second, and fourth verses of "Onward, Christian Soldiers."

I survived the rock and roll era. My favorites are still the "oldies," although that means different things to different people. Someone said that in 40 years rap music would be the "oldies." I tune into the "somebody done me wrong songs" of country music. Remembering the first time I heard Johnny Cash sing "Ring of Fire," I marvel at his deep bass voice. I still sing parts of that song.

Like most kids, I learned my ABCs singing the alphabet song. People remember the words of a song easier than simply memorizing facts. Just look at what the TV shows like *Sesame Street* taught America's children.

In darkest times, people have turned to music to lift their spirits. Music continues to raise the hopes of the hopeless. Jazz, swing, and

Dixieland tunes helped people through the Great Depression years of the 1930s, and the poorest of Americans could listen to singers like Louis Armstrong and his generation of music makers.

Even though I had the opportunity to experience voice, piano, organ, guitar, banjo, and violin lessons, I didn't practice any of them long enough, or learn to play any of them well enough to use them with skill today.

Hard times and struggle birthed the soulful sounds of the blues. BB King and his guitar named "Lucille" set those blues into song. Big bands and their singers sparked a whole new generation of music forming the standards. Today I like to set channel 937 of TV music to the "Singers and Standards," relax with Frank Sinatra and Dinah Shore, and ponder how time and circumstances change our music. Today there are no musical variety shows. My parents always tuned the TV to Lawrence Welk on Saturday nights.

The upbeat rhythms of Latin music offer good listening, and bring festival, dancing, and celebration to the music. I listen even without understanding a word.

Who doesn't love holiday music? Christmas songs abound through the month of December. There's "Auld Lang Syne" for bringing in a new year full of possibilities. There are wonderful Easter songs to celebrate the resurrection of our Savior. In addition, there are breathtaking patriotic songs on July 4 when we celebrate the independence of America, and others that tell of its majestic beauty from sea to shining sea.

Generations of creative musicians and songwriters come and go. In spite of Don McLean's "American Pie" belief that music died with Buddy Holly, music is far from dead; more singers, songwriters, and musicians are born every day.

My collection of music includes a stack of vinyl records and a pile of eight-track tapes. Evolving technology enhances our love for music. Recording sound developed from Edison's tinfoil cylinder to the finest, flawless sounds emitting from woofers and tweeters. I recently listened to an old sound bite recorded in the early twentieth century. Scratchy sounds overpowered and drowned out the soloists words to "The Old Grey Mare."

We hum along to our favorite movie theme songs. Who can forget the haunting tune from the movie *Jaws*, "do doomph do doomph." And remember all the TV show theme songs? I still sing the theme from the *Beverly Hillbillies*.

People want their music to be mobile and load their iPods with favorite songs to carry along for a jog, bike ride, or walk. We download songs from the internet, and play them on our PCs, MP3 players, and cell phones. Teenagers with earphones stuck in their ears bounce to the beat of the latest songs.

Television wants in on the evolution of music and creates reality shows to discover the next *American Idol*. Americans turn their favorite music artists into icons and worship them like idols. Yes, there is both good and bad in music.

The air is alive with the sounds of music—literally. Thousands of radio stations broadcast all conceivable venues of music into the air, AM, FM, and digital, as our brains resonate to these proffered frequencies.

Music helps us express ourselves. With the advent of karaoke, we can sing like wannabe celebrities and use the notes even when we don't have the right words. Music has brought us through wars and unrest. We sing of love, hate, peace, and revolution. Music makes us happy, makes us sad, inspires us, and revolts us. Music carries messages and sets a mood for special moments.

Everyone relates to music, and each has a story; mine is only one. From easy listening to hard rock, one-person vocals to grand stage presentations, radio to records, CD to iPod, there is no doubt that America loves its music.

~ Jack Elder

THE PLACE I BELONG

*"Country roads, take me home
to the place I belong..."*
—John Denver

The magic was back. Astride Papa's big brown horse, I felt almost giddy with excitement as my brothers and I rode through the pecan trees of our grandfather's farm. We could hear the nuts crunching underfoot as we wandered around unsupervised (or so we thought). Wanting more space, I guided my horse carefully down a red clay embankment, avoiding the deep ruts, and then smiled as a wide field spread before us. Now I could trot!

Riding horses was just one of the many treats I enjoyed when visiting my grandparents in Cordele, Georgia. A suburbanite, I left the big city a few weeks every year and reveled in small town life. Where else could my brothers and I saunter down to the railroad tracks and pick blackberries for hours? Or walk down the street to the Little League ballpark all lit up on summer nights? And where else could we swing on a wide and welcoming wraparound porch where relatives would rock and chat over iced tea?

I remember happily pounding out hymns on Mama's old upright piano in the dining room while breathing in the lemony fragrance of magnolia blossoms on the sideboard. Every meal was a labor of love, and the food delectable. I'd wake up every morning to spread my breakfast toast with Mama's luscious pear or fig preserves, and in the midday dinner sampled tomato aspic, collard greens, and homemade pickled peaches. The food seemed special at Mama's and Papa's.

Those carefree days in Cordele were just a pleasant foretaste of life in another small town many years later with my husband and daughter. A new job brought us to Abingdon nestled in the Blue Ridge Mountains of Virginia. Just as Jan Karon's Mitford endeared her readers to "the little town with the big heart," so Abingdon won us over with its warmth and charm.

Located in the southwest corner of the state, the town was founded in 1778. Pioneers heading west in covered wagons trekked through the center of town on the Great Wagon Road, now called Main Street. Long before that, legend has it that Daniel Boone's dogs were attacked by wolves in a cave, and he named the area "Wolf Hills." This name stuck until the town was renamed Abingdon for Martha Washington's ancestral home in England. To commemorate the original name, iron wolf statues stand guard outside many public buildings.

Tourists frequent the famous Barter Theater, where patrons used to swap produce for a ticket during Depression days. A family of eight once traded a piglet for their admission. Across the street from the theatre stands the Martha Washington Inn, another downtown landmark. This stately southern mansion, once a private residence, was a women's college for 70 years. During the Civil War, the buildings were used as a training barracks for the Washington Mounted Rifles, commanded by Captain William E. "Grumble" Jones. In 1935, the building reopened as the Martha Washington Inn, now a five-star hotel furnished with priceless antiques from a gentler era.

Just as in the old days, time in Abingdon seems to slow its relentless pace and people take time for one another. Soon after we had moved into our house, a succession of four neighbors brought steaming dishes and welcoming smiles to our door. Their generosity overwhelmed me. Another unexpected delight was the way pedestrians on the sidewalks often waved to us as we drove by. We felt valued and affirmed. Even grocery shopping was pleasant as fellow shoppers, who didn't seem to be in a hurry, acknowledged my presence and smiled. Our three-year-old, Laura, would sometimes greet approaching shoppers with a sweet, "Hi, honey!" (My greeting when she awoke from her naps). People would stop short, and then grin as they met her big blue eyes. She was a natural icebreaker.

Regardless of a town's culture, though, nothing can take the place of finding the right church home. Abingdon Bible Church enfolded us with acceptance and love. Our family was invited to join a Friday night home Bible study; talking, praying, and singing together brought us near the others. In addition, a neighborhood friend included me in a local ladies' Bible study group. As we shared our lives with one another, my newcomer awkwardness eased. Later on when Laura was five, our church began an Awana program. As I led the singing and helped the children learn their memory verses, I knew we were investing in the next generation.

Besides our church activities, Mark and I loved the natural beauty of the area and plunged into various outdoor adventures. A short bike ride from our house was a lovely walking/biking trail that wound its way through dense woods with rolling fields beckoning from either side. Formerly railroad tracks, the Virginia Creeper Trail was named for the train that steamed slowly through the knobs and farmlands for fifty years. The last locomotive to make the trek is on display at the trail head in Abingdon.

But bike riding wasn't as exciting as climbing mountains, so my husband Mark took lessons for two years with Edge of the World Outfitters in Banner Elk, North Carolina. As the name implies, the sport is not for the fainthearted, his wife included. Sometimes I watched him scale Backbone Rock, but I preferred the lower elevations. When Mark decided to teach our five-year-old how to rappel off a 30-foot rock face at Grayson Highlands State Park, I watched as he carefully secured Laura on the rope. The climbing bug bit her too, and she's enjoyed the challenge ever since.

    The year Laura learned to rappel, my brother and his family relocated from Atlanta to our neighborhood, three houses down. As an extra blessing, they also attended our church. Abingdon felt more like home than ever with our extended family so close. Many times Laura and her two-year-old cousin would play together while I chatted with my sister-in-law. We enjoyed several festivals with them, sipping cider at Grayson Highlands, sampling maple syrup at White Top Mountain, and shopping for crafts at the famous Virginia Highlands Festival in the summer.

    Hot air balloon launches cap off the last weekend of the celebration. I'll never forget the Saturday mornings I was jolted awake by strange sounds, and then relaxed as I recognized the huffing, hissing sound of hot air balloons drifting just over our house. We threw on some clothes and raced outdoors in time to watch the colorful globes floating by overhead. Eight or ten balloons filled the sky, each one a bright collage of patterns and hues. I would always think of the *Wizard of Oz* when the professor was helplessly borne aloft shouting, "I can't come back! I don't know how it works!"

Just like the professor, our family also had to leave, reluctantly. In May of 1992, Mark returned to work in Atlanta. Laura and I had a little more time to say goodbye as we tried to sell our house. By November, though, we joined Mark in Atlanta and the house sold soon thereafter. Leaving Abingdon was one of the hardest things we've ever done. We still visit our friends there every few years, and whenever we do, it's always like coming home.

~ Mary Bowen

AN AMERICAN CHILDHOOD

Likes and dislikes, habits and patterns, gifts and talents, quirks and idiosyncrasies ... we all have them ... but how did we develop such things? What keeps one person neat and organized while another never seems to figure out where anything should go or how to get it in place and make it stay there? What makes one individual love nature and being out-of-doors while another is content to look at nature through a bay window while seated inside in a comfortable chair? What makes one person pursue one adventure after another in life, while another is perfectly happy to read about adventure in a fast-paced book?

Although God created all of us with certain gifts, talents, and bents, we must admit, the way we were brought up in America—our family and cultural values during the era of our individual childhoods—contributed a great deal to making us who we are today.

I grew up during the 1950s and '60s in a Christian home with two parents who unconditionally loved the Lord, one another, my brother, and me. I spent my childhood in small Mississippi and Louisiana towns where the highlight of each week was spending time with family and friends at home, at school, and at church. I heard little about crime and danger. My only encounter with death came with the passing of my two grandfathers, who both died of illnesses during my junior high school days.

I led a blessed and sheltered life and consequently took many things for granted. I never worried about whether my parents loved me. Their actions proved they did. I never worried about having food, clothing, or a place to live. Those things were provided for me daily and unconditionally. I never struggled with family relationships or with friendships, since by nature I was a "people person" who made friends easily. I enjoyed school and learning new things, and I loved going to church and learning about the Lord. I accepted Jesus Christ as my Savior at the age of 10, and dedicated my life to full-time Christian service when I turned 18. I have walked in faith ever since.

Because of those blessings, my memories are usually enjoyable and fun-filled. Actually, I find it quite fascinating to look back and see how the personality characteristics I carry today developed through my childhood. Those who know me well know that I'm a dedicated bargain shopper, an avid collector, and am by nature somewhat competitive and driven. Those characteristics developed in my early childhood when I learned three important facts: there were things you could get for free, some things came in sets and you could collect all of them, and you got rewarded for being the best at whatever you did.

When I was very young, I loved picking wild onion bouquets for my mother and my grandmothers. I also loved picking up pecans at my dad's parents' house and digging for fishing worms at my mom's parents' house. You see ... all of those things—wildflowers, pecans, and worms—were absolutely free. No one even minded how many of them I collected. Life just couldn't have gotten any better than that!

The summer before I entered second grade, we moved from Natchez, Mississippi into a small neighborhood in Vidalia, Louisiana. Behind our property stretched a huge field filled with red clover. It delighted me when I found out that no one cared if I picked as many of those beautiful flowers (or should we say weeds) as I wanted to pick. I added vases and vases of red clover blossoms to my bunches of wild onions. I'm sure my mother, grandmothers, and favorite neighbors were thrilled to receive those weed bouquets!

In the middle of that clover field, facing the main highway that ran parallel to our street, sat a huge Bill-Ups Service Station—a station that offered a large variety of stuffed animals for sale. Every time I went with my dad to get gas at Bill-Ups, I drooled over those critters. I begged my dad week after week to buy me one, but since he didn't have a lot of spare cash and also firmly believed that things earned were far more appreciated and cared for than things received as gifts, he suggested that I save my allowance so I could buy a stuffed animal for myself.

Though I wasn't too thrilled about the wait, I took my dad up on his suggestion. After working, scrimping, saving, and searching regularly under sofa cushions, I finally managed to buy myself a stuffed critter—a huge red dog that remained one of my favorites until long after I had gone off to college. (I'd probably still have that dog and many other stuffed animals had my parents not "gotten rid of the junk" when they moved to another city while I was away at college.)

That dog began my love affair with collecting plush. I collected stuffed animals all through my elementary, junior, and senior high days. After I married and had children, I even used my children as an excuse to continue buying those soft, cuddly creatures. And needless to say, by the time my awesome grandchildren came along, I was a lost cause as week after week I shopped for stuffed critters and Beanie Babies™ to add to their collections—and mine.

Stuffed animals weren't the only thing I collected in great numbers during childhood. My parents were both smokers, so mother often bought boxes of individual matchbooks. Those matchbooks came with beautiful covers decorated with different varieties of birds, flowers, and wildlife. I couldn't wait for Mother and Daddy to use up each book of matches so I could add it to my collection. I kept those empty matchbooks for years.

During junior high years, I added many postcards, glass animal figurines, and silver charms for my bracelet to my collections. I also competed with a friend to see who could collect the most four-leaf clovers, which I pressed into my Pony Tail scrapbook alongside my post card collection. (I also had the matching Pony Tail wallet and diary.) I still have my childhood collection of charms, my Pony Tail scrapbook and diary, and a number of the figurines.

And then there were the doll collections. I still have dolls I collected during my childhood years, as well as dolls I purchased for my three daughters when they were growing up. Although my girls loved dolls—Strawberry Shortcake, Cabbage Patch Kids, Barbie with all her accessories, and more—they didn't love them enough to take them along when they grew up, married, and moved away. Instead, they asked me to keep them at my house. Those dolls are housed in five large doll cases and line the tops of bookcases. In addition are my collections of fast food toys, old cameras, kitchen antiques, children's books and other collectible publications, as well as multiple varieties of seashells.

During my childhood, I began my life-long quest to build huge collections and also developed my competitive spirit. As soon as I was old enough to understand games, I played jacks, marbles, Chinese Checkers, and board games like Monopoly, Sorry, and Clue. I hated to lose at anything, so I spent lots of time practicing and building my skills. To this day, I still have a collection of marbles, and I love to play board games.

I spent the remainder of my childhood watching the Mickey Mouse Club, Shirley Temple, Captain Kangaroo, Lassie, Tarzan, Saturday morning cartoons, and The Wonderful World of Disney on TV, riding my bicycle, skating, and playing paper dolls. To earn money to support my collecting habit, I made colorful loop potholders, which I sold door to door and also sold copies of an American publication called *Grit* magazine.

    Yes, I can count growing up in America during the 1950s and '60s a tremendous blessing and privilege ... and oh, how I wish I could leave today's fast-paced lifestyle and go back in time to bring that way of life back for my children and grandchildren to enjoy. They just don't know what they missed!

~ Diana J. Baker

LEAF DAY REMEMBERED

As I settled onto my porch swing, coffee cup in hand, I gazed at the giant oak tree in my front yard. Bare, gnarled limbs were silhouetted against the cloudless sky. The little mountain range at the end of the Appalachian chain formed a beautiful backdrop for its expansive branches. Looking over the valley, I noticed the steam from my coffee mirrored a whisk of smoke rising from down the lane.

The air was crisp and still, almost as if the earth were holding its breath. Nothing moved, and the quiet was almost audible. As I nudged the swing into gentle motion, something quickened my senses. The unmistakable whiff of burning leaves wafted down my little country road. Suddenly I was transported to another time. Nearly sixty years evaporated as memories of other fall days flooded my consciousness.

Seasons in the plains of Nebraska had no blurred edges. Scorching temperatures remained until the end of September. School was miserable on those days as small oscillating fans worked overtime, but failed to bring relief to our sweltering classrooms. Rivulets of sweat trickled down our brows and necks as we romped on the playground. In the late afternoons, toward the end of the month, we swapped out shorts for jeans as we tried to squeeze out a bit more playtime from the quickly cooling days. Fall brought a welcome but brief respite, before the bleak winter months would lock us indoors.

Then one morning the moms up and down the block would call us back inside for a sweater before we headed to school. When we dashed home after school to change into play clothes, we'd discover all our shorts and sandals were boxed up, ready to move to the attic. Instead, we found last year's flannel shirts hanging in the closet. We were told to throw one on over a T-shirt before we could head outside. What a nuisance! The flapping material caught on everything because we couldn't button the too-short sleeves, and we lost valuable playtime trying to keep them rolled up above our elbows.

Soon, once another payday arrived, Dad would drive us to Sears for new clothes. I was guaranteed two new shirts because I was the oldest. By the time we made it to the store, I would have ripped at least one sleeve. Mom could patch our clothes well so my younger sister, Diane, would end up with one old, one ratty, and one new flannel shirt. Seems there were only three colors for kids' plaid flannel shirts: red, green, and blue. Because Diane was getting only one, she was allowed to choose first. No matter what, I knew I'd be stuck with the green one.

I really needed new jeans too. Unfortunately, I only grew up, not out, so my pants still fit at the waist. I'd have to wait a couple more paydays before I could ditch my high-waders. Every week more of my socks would show! My weird looking clothes didn't slow me down much, though. Most every kid on the block endured seasonal wardrobe malfunctions.

Saturdays were filled with sandlot baseball as we reenacted Big League play-off games. You could overhear heated sidewalk conversations as fans defended their favorite teams. Every male proudly donned a franchise cap and loudly expressed opinions about contested plays. Once, when the series championship was locked in a tie, we were allowed to do deskwork at school as we listened to that final game. We had to promise to keep the cheering down as we strained to listen to the nearly inaudible broadcast. Other classes weren't as privileged. We had the cool teacher who smuggled in a tabletop radio. It was a perfect day. We enjoyed something deliciously forbidden *and* the Yankees won.

Too soon, Leaf Day arrived. You could always tell when it had come. Neighborhood dads hauled rakes, tarps, and wheelbarrows out of basements and garages. The air would be decidedly crisp. By eleven o'clock, our breath didn't produce little puffs of vapor any more. In the Midwest, this time usually occurred around the middle of October. Only the outrageously fastidious tackled their yards before the winds blew the last leaves off the trees.

Fall was my very favorite time of the year. I loved walking to school scuffing my feet to make the leaves dance up before me. I particularly enjoyed running into the miniature prairie whirlwinds to insinuate myself amongst the swirling leaves. Before that fateful day in October, the elms, poplars, maples, and oaks flaunted riotous color. Bronze, gold, yellow, red, and orange leaves would float lazily to the ground; only to be lifted high again as the wind blustered down the street. The pelting leaves created the illusion of being inside a kaleidoscope. I loved being bombarded by those lovely missiles as I battled the wind. I weighed so little and it would knock me sideways as I walked home from school.

Oh how I hated to see tattered leaves turn a bleak brown and litter the yards. Yet the denuded trees brought new revelations. Bare branches revealed an awesome beauty. Thick trunks supported huge gnarled branches, and sturdy limbs with tiny fingers uplifted in a kind of worship. I felt very small making my way past the silent majestic sentinels. When I looked up, I knew that after the winter's rest, each little twig would send forth new growth, creating a canopy of green that would whisper in the wind. Next fall, we could once again celebrate the circle of life with more bonfires and roasted marshmallows.

On Leaf Day, Saturday chores were quickly completed and everyone headed outside. Diane and I had to start in the corners of our yard and rake everything onto a tarp. Mom cleaned behind the shrubs and Daddy hauled the ladder out to tackle the task of cleaning the gutters. I hated the job of raking up all those icky clumps of gloppy leaves that Dad dropped from the gutters above. Up and down the street, families were working on the same chores and leaf piles continued to grow higher.

One year someone got the idea to create a gigantic leaf pile under the tree in my front yard. We figured we could make it so tall that we could jump off the lowest branches to our leaf mountain without risking our own limbs. Soon kids were hauling leaves in bushel baskets from their yards to ours. We managed to build the pile to a mound above our heads. It was the best day ever. I felt invincible as I propelled myself through the air to land on the crest, then tumble down the slope to the ground. Leaves stuck in my hair, got inside my shirt, and up my pants legs.

We whooped and hollered as we launched ourselves into the air. Even the little kids grew daring as we boosted them up into the tree, then swung them down to the leaf pile where big brothers or sisters waited to catch them. After our play break, the dad-whistles called us all back to work. Miraculously, everyone helped me haul our community mound of leaves to my backyard before returning to their own homes and chores.

Soon tendrils of smoke rose skyward as piles of leaves were ignited. Hoses snaked through backyards and into the alley so the grassy verge could be continuously dampened. Diane and I liked to drag our leaf-laden tarp to the smoldering pit beyond our backyard and masterfully empty it without dousing the flames. Dumping all the leaves at once could put the fire out. The trick was to carefully let the leaves trickle off the tarp. After the last load was cleared, the reward for our labor was a marshmallow roast. Toward dusk, the air around us was replete with the smoke from dozens of alleyway fires. Sparks from the glowing embers flitted upward as kids stirred the flames. When the chill in the air began making our teeth chatter, moms marched us inside for baths, then bed.

Leaf Day marked the termination of those endless hours of outdoor play. Winter was fast approaching, but any fallen leaves that remained had a final use. One neighbor, Mr. Sundstrum, maintained a big pile of these leaves until the temperatures dropped below freezing. We all helped create a giant leaf circle. Then he would gradually dampen it down until it froze solid. A few days later, he would flood the center and create an ice skating rink for us. Every weekend we would strap on the skates and practice spins and figure eights. By the time the pond at our local park froze over, we'd be ready for races and a game of crack the whip.

A noisy flock of migrating blackbirds landed in my yard, breaking my reverie and bringing me back to the present. Looking over our two acres of front lawn, I was exceedingly thankful my husband, Dick, availed himself of a lawnmower that could chop and/or bag leaves. I wondered if families still observed Leaf Day, and if children have to give up a Saturday to prepare the lawn for winter. Still thinking of those fun days of my childhood, I headed indoors and "nuked" a cup of water for hot chocolate with marshmallows on top. Some things improve with the passing of time.

~ Linda Hayes

THE EDGE OF INNOCENCE

Growing up in the South during the late '60s, I was raised on the edge of innocence. The simple joys I learned from my grandparents would become a strong foundation for dealing with life as it unfolded around me. The years ahead would bring the sexual revolution, an unprecedented number of divorces, and crime rates that would alter the open society that America once held dear. Brass locks that decorated my grandparent's doors served no real function. I never once heard a knock at the door. All of their friends just waltzed in as if they were part of the family—and indeed, they were.

In most modern day neighborhoods, strangers live next door, but in the era of my grandparents, it was hard to find anyone you did not know. I can remember fidgeting impatiently when a five-minute trip to buy fishing bait turned into a thirty-minute conversation with someone my grandfather had not seen in a whole month. He never made it out of any business without a lengthy conversation.

As a young boy, my greatest cares were getting out of school without homework and hoping it wouldn't rain when I wanted to fish. I heard my mother talking to Grandma about my uncle being sent to Vietnam, but in my mind, that was a military base somewhere near Marietta, Georgia, where they visited him as he prepared for his deployment.

My grandfather was known to everyone as "Pappy." He loved to tell corny jokes. They were the kind of jokes that made you want to roll your eyes. He took great pleasure in drawing that reaction from people, and he would tell the same jokes at every opportunity. If someone laughed, he enjoyed a good laugh with them. If they didn't laugh, he enjoyed a good laugh at their pained expression.

Few things were more thrilling than Pappy saying to me, "Come on. I'm gonna learn you how to fish." Sometimes those lessons were painful. One time I hooked a large fish and he rushed over to give me step-by-step instructions. "Hold your rod up," he kept ordering. I was standing on a large flat rock that the fish had rushed under for refuge. I reached out with my rod to keep the line from rubbing against the jagged surface. "Hold your rod up, hold your rod up."

I tried to explain that I had to keep the line away from the sharp rock. Unfazed, he continued to issue the same order, "Hold your rod up!" Pappy had a stubborn streak and I don't think I ever heard him change his mind, even when facing a mountain of contradicting evidence. On this occasion, I grew irritated and decided to follow his orders even though I knew it would break my line. I held my rod up, and my line sliced across the rock as the fish sought for a path of escape. The rod sprang up as an empty line floated lazily in the breeze. Pappy said that it wouldn't have snapped if I had only followed his instructions.

As far as I can remember, that is the only time I let his orders get the best of me. Everyone loved Pappy, but no one could work with him—no one except me. Whether it was fishing or working, Pappy felt the need to instruct whomever he was working with. Because of the great love he always expressed for me, I learned how to say, "Okay" when he barked instructions, even when it was something already being done. I soon found that I enjoyed working with him, in spite of this quirk.

Each school year, I longed for summer vacation when I could go spend a week or two with my grandparents. Pappy showed me every good fishing spot on the Yellow River that flowed near his house in Porterdale, Georgia. It was a delight to come back with a mess of fish. Pappy would say, "You can't go inside until we get these fish cleaned."

One day, we were just finishing up with this chore and I had been watching a catfish head with his mouth wide open. For reasons unknown, I decided to put my finger in the mouth of that fish. When I touched its tongue, the jaws clamped down hard on my finger and its strength caught me off guard. I screamed as the vice-like mouth crushed my finger. Pappy walked over with two screwdrivers and pried the jaws apart, freeing my finger.

With a sly look, Pappy asked, "What did you go and do that fer? What did you think was going to happen?" I shrugged, but I wanted to tell him that I thought fish heads wouldn't have the strength to fight back.

My grandfather fished all year long and stored all our catches in a large chest freezer. In the early fall, he would have a big fish fry that was more of a celebration of life than a meal. My Uncle Henry would hook up his propane fryer and it seemed like the entire town of Porterdale would come out. We would all sit under the large pecan trees at my uncle's house and enjoy hot fish in the cool shade.

Uncle Henry was a big man who loved to show off his strength. After the feeding frenzy subsided, he would go to his barn and bring out his relics of brawn. He had two large semicircle magnets that clamped tightly together. He would pass them around and challenge all the men to try pulling them apart. Every man there would strain, twist, and pull against the magnets until someone would utter the words Henry longed to hear, "I don't think those things can come apart."

That was always Uncle Henry's cue. He would take the magnets and say, "Watch this." Each of his large hands would wrap around one of the magnets and then this big man would try his best to keep his face from showing any strain as he pulled the magnets apart. He would smile and hold up the separated halves for all to see, and then put them back together with a loud snap. He would hand the magnets over to a challenger for another vain effort, amplifying the magnitude of his feat.

The men's conversation centered on church life, their hunting dogs, and where the fish were jumping. The women folk took turns cranking the hand-turned ice cream maker while they talked about men, their kids, and where they found the best bargains. We tried to avoid this area, but when the ladies tired of cranking, they would fetch the kids to help with this task. I'm not sure which was worse, the pain in my arm as I cranked the handle, or the disappointment of missing the conversations among the men. The joy of finding a ten-dollar sweater for three dollars was not my idea of exciting talk.

Rarely did one of these gatherings end without Pappy getting out his guitar to play hymns. The families would reunite into a large circle as we ate homemade banana ice cream and sang about the "Sweet Bye and Bye." While the strumming of the guitar followed the tune of the old hymns, Pappy sang in a key that never quite matched. As everyone joined in for this country cantata, voices rang out like clanking keys, but everyone smiled in harmony, unaware of their voices clashing in the air.

As my grandparent's generation receded into the past, my generation emerged to witness many changes in our American culture. When I was a child, there was no fear of walking down the street at night and violent acts shocked the nation. But as Atlanta became a city with one of the nation's highest crime rates, doors became locked in the daytime, and children played under the watchful eyes of parents.

I am thankful I was born on the edge of innocence, and see it as my duty to carry part of it into the next generation. In childhood, I had one foot in the generation of innocence, and in adulthood, the other foot in the receding morality of a post-Christian culture. With gratitude, I remember this era my generation almost missed.

That era in American history may have been forgotten by our modern culture, but I remember and cherish those days. Days when simple pleasures gave me a sweet taste of life. The work was hard, luxuries were few, but people and communities were close. I'm grateful that I lived during a time when I could glimpse the innocence of life my grandparents enjoyed. It continues to live in my heart, and I seek to teach my children how they can carry their part of America's innocence into the next generation.

~ Eddie Snipes

LONG MARCH TO FORT SILL

The waning afternoon sun, partially obscured by railroad smoke, threw a few searching beams upon Morris Street. It was a dusty side street intersecting Howell Mill Road, not far from the Atlanta Water Works. Six dingy gray houses fronted one side of Morris Street, opposite a maze of railroad sidings with lonely freight cars awaiting relocation.

Ledford and Nelly Ames leased one of these tiny frame houses. The late June sky looked like tarnished gold, and the air was hot and dry. Tobias, the Ames' only child who was known as "Toby," was playing army in the backyard when he heard the sudden loud crashing sounds.

He ran the familiar path to the front gate, as his oversized army helmet bounced on his head. Holding his rifle in one hand, Toby unfastened the gate with the other, and then dashed across a narrow sidewalk. As he took cover behind a large wooden telephone pole with its sticky sides smelling strongly of creosote in the heat, his eyes watered uncontrollably.

Catching his breath, he peered around the large pole. *Yes*, he thought, *the bad guys are in that red boxcar with the open doors.* A big black switch engine was revving its motors as it rolled along shiny tracks, sounding like a powerful roaring furnace that whirled inside an echo chamber. It backed slowly and coupled with the boxcar, making a tremendous crash. Toby fired his toy rifle rapidly at six imaginary foes. Three of them fell from the boxcar while the others ducked back out of sight. The huge engine moved off with a metallic screech. He watched, forlorn, as the three remaining enemies escaped, lurking inside the boxcar's dark shadows.

As the rattling noise subsided, Toby heard his mother's voice calling from beyond the battlefield. "Toby, how many times have we told you to stay inside the fence? It's dangerous near this street and you must stay away from those trains. Come in, your dad will be home for supper soon."

"Ah, Mom," he said. "It's hard to spot bad guys from inside an old fence." Toby shuffled through the wooden gate she held open for him. She wrapped her son in a big hug as he squirmed to get loose. Smiling back at his pretty mother, he dashed to the back yard to watch for stray cats.

A week later, the Ames family moved from Morris Street to Fourteenth Street into a small drab garage apartment, just behind an old brick apartment building. For a few months, Toby attended first grade at Spring Street Elementary. There, students played with simple musical instruments, sat in groups as the teachers read stories to them, took afternoon naps at their desks, and ate box lunches of sandwiches and potato chips brought from home. Cartons of milk were available for ten cents. But in less than a year, and before Toby could get used to his new routine, his family moved again.

  This time Toby's parents purchased a vintage brick house on Brookwood Drive, about a mile south of Buckhead. Toby attended Garden Hills Elementary School where his teacher, Charlotte Bagwell, made learning fun and interesting. He participated in skits about George Washington and Abe Lincoln. Honor was valued, and this plus other character traits were taught to the children.

  The school's band director, Norah Sisk, was tall, attractive, and enthusiastic. She talked to Toby's mother and explained why she recommended the clarinet. "His mouth is shaped right for woodwinds, which we need; and I can suggest a tutor." So, after school, Toby began taking private clarinet lessons from Mr. Edwards, the principal of a nearby high school.

  After eight lessons, Toby was allowed to join a four-school band called the Northside Highlander Elementary Band. He was thrilled by the music they played, and especially loved the marches made popular by John Philip Sousa. Under Mrs. Sisk's enthusiastic direction, those martial songs made everyone feel like marching out to battle. Each time the band performed, the young musicians were inspired and played with gusto. When a concert was over, parents and friends applauded vigorously. Communities were close-knit in those days.

Toby loved music. He took advanced clarinet lessons from a member of the Atlanta symphony. His parents purchased an upright piano and hired Mrs. Matilda Hess, on Fourteenth Street, to give their son lessons. She owned a gleaming black Steinway grand piano with real ivory keys. Toby enjoyed taking his instruction there. Mrs. Hess played the piano beautifully with her long, powerful fingers dancing over the keys. Toby thought his piano teacher's hands appeared strong; the blue veins stood out prominently in them as she played. He sat next to her on a large padded piano bench of dark blue leather. When he played his lessons well, she decorated his music sheets with colorful stars.

Years later Nelly Ames asked her son, "Toby, how did you memorize all those notes in Beethoven's *Sonata Pathetique*? I have trouble remembering what's in my favorite recipes."

"I don't know, Mom," Toby replied. "The notes just seem to be in my fingers."

Summer vacation without school and homework was the best. Toby loved swimming and went to a nearby public pool almost every day. In the deep end near the diving board, he would search the pool bottom for hairpins and coins. He had to be careful about divers coming from above. Occasionally, the lifeguard blew his loud whistle to clear the pool.

On hot summer days in the South, he and his friends would meet to ride their bikes fast, speeding uphill then coasting down to catch a breeze. His English-made bike had gears, which helped on long hills.

At their favorite drug store was a soda fountain. There, boys and girls would have a cherry lime freeze or a coke with cherry. Ice cream cones were only five cents for a single dip, and ten cents for a double scoop.

It was a time of childish abandon, Little League baseball, and flying kites on windy days. Toby was athletic. He played centerfield in baseball and loved other sports. Flying a kite over a sloping grassy field with no power lines was calming and a favorite thing to do. His spirits rose as the kite climbed high in the blue sky, hoping to touch the fluffy white clouds. Those were innocent times. He made friends easily, felt secure, trusted people, and did not worry.

In his early teen years, Toby and his parents moved yet again. His dad and uncles achieved success in the furniture business. Now during summer breaks, Toby worked at one of the family stores delivering furniture. As the family business prospered, the Ames built a new house in a nicer neighborhood.

At Northside High, he encountered a different atmosphere. Toby made his first "C" and his teachers seemed autocratic and uninterested in their students. He liked rock and roll music and let his hair grow long. Sports coaches and teachers frowned on long hair and Toby's grades continued to drop. He and his few friends were considered rebels.

Concerned friends suggested that Toby's parents send him to a good military school. Ultimately, that decision was made and for the next two years, Toby suffered the regimented life of a cadet. During this time, his grades did improve, but he still felt insecure and lonely. After military school, he enrolled with high hopes in a Baptist college.

Toby sang in the college glee club and hoped to succeed in his academic studies, but he was unsure of his strengths and he lacked substantial goals. Two years later he joined a fraternity where "frat" brothers joked that earning a "gentleman's C" was quite acceptable.

Knowing something of military life, he enrolled in the Reserves Officer Training Corps (ROTC) all four years of college. He was elected Captain (the highest rank) of the Pershing Rifles Drill Team, and was proud when they were selected to march in the inauguration parade for John F. Kennedy, our nation's 35th president.

One day, Ledford Ames had a talk with Toby, who had such potential but seemed apathetic, "Son, if you don't know what to major in, why not try business. You can always use it." Toby remembered how his father and uncles had succeeded in business without the benefit of college.

While Toby continued with college, he majored in business, but his teachers did not make the subjects come alive for him. One professor, nicknamed "Yogi," sat on top of his desk cross-legged, rubbing his head of prickly hair and droning on about his various economic *theories*. It seemed that most of the business professors had little or no practical business experience.

After investing four more years of his life at this college, Toby did not graduate. He knew it was his fault and felt guilty for wasting his parents' money and hopes. In disgrace, he tried to pick up the pieces and began working as a computer operator for an Atlanta-based banking institution. Toby took a few college night classes, but he felt beaten down and weary. For a young man, he was in very poor health.

Americans had fought in Korea and our nation was now at war in Vietnam. First, Toby withdrew from school and then was drafted and sent for U.S. Army Basic Training at Fort Benning, Georgia. He entered the Army feeling humiliated, but quickly made a remarkable recovery. He built a rock garden for the First Sergeant and scored high on math tests, then was reassigned to Ft. Sill, Oklahoma where he studied field artillery. Classes about artillery cannons and gunnery and fire direction centers excited him. He qualified for Officer Candidate School (OCS). After advanced individual artillery training, he went through six long months of artillery OCS. He fired a variety of weapons and learned leadership skills.

Finally, he graduated and felt like nobility as one of only half the fifty candidates in the artillery battery that had successfully completed OCS training. Although Toby's parents were not present that day, he would see them on his Christmas leave before being shipped overseas. He felt guilty for his past failures, but while other men dodged the draft and hid in Canada, he stepped up to serve his country proudly. It was a second chance, and he knew this time he would succeed.

~ Marcus Beavers

THROUGH THE EYES OF OLD GLORY

At least the museum was air-conditioned, and I was glad to sit down at the little desk in the corner, but the job was so boring! The hand-painted murals on the walls depicted all of the major U.S. wars. Every wall was covered in scenes that transitioned—one to another—with picture book quality. Some of the scenes were violent and bloody, and showed soldiers screaming in horror as they fought for their lives.

As a recent college graduate with the world at my feet, I hated war and my leanings were very liberal. I felt that any country's disagreements should be settled with a game of chess, or perhaps football, to decide the issue at hand, but not by people fighting in a war. In the very early '80s, patriotism was not "cool" in some circles. The popular television show, M.A.S.H., had just ended its long-running series leaving me in strong agreement with one of the characters, "Hawkeye," that war was *unnecessary*.

My dad had secured this summer job for me since he had been instrumental in the building of the War Memorial and Military Museum in our hometown, Gadsden, Alabama. He had been so proud the day of the ribbon cutting, giving a speech in his Army "dress blues." He had seemed reserved, as if he were speaking at a funeral, yet in some way happier than I had ever seen him. I did not understand his emotional highs and lows.

That summer was a unique opportunity for me to get to know my dad better, but I didn't realize it until I looked back on this time many years later. While sending out resumes and searching for my dream job in corporate America, I worked as a summer assistant in this place filled with images of war. Dad and I met over coffee each morning as we worked the crossword puzzle in the daily paper. I didn't know it then, but this would be my best summer ever, and for so many reasons.

At the museum, I studied the mural paintings for many hours and for many days. Nearly thirty years later, I can still recall those scenes in tremendously vivid detail, especially the eyes of the soldiers who seemed only moments from death. It stirred my soul. These paintings were so dramatic and realistic; I could almost hear the pain screaming from the walls. Without a doubt, the artist had created an incredible work of imagery, but I only thought of how much I hated the job and anything related to war.

One dull afternoon some guests walked in for a tour—an older couple, their adult son and his wife, and a 12-year-old grandson. They had driven a long way, and they remained in the museum for hours, slowly taking in the displays while examining each panel of war scenes. It was obvious the young boy was interested. He seemed to associate the different war times with what he had learned in his history classes. I could see that the murals were teaching him more about the wars. The illustrations put faces to the words in his history books.

    The World War II section was a bit larger than the other wars. I noticed the older man stood there for close to an hour. He started talking to me about it and I found myself telling him about my dad, who served in the Army Air Corps. It sparked his interest and he excitedly asked me several questions that, to my dismay, I could not answer.

    When they left, he shook my hand and asked me to thank my dad for his efforts—for remembering and honoring all the soldiers. This recognition made the sacrifice worth it, he explained, by enabling others to look back and know they fought to keep America safe.

    Instead of rolling my eyes and scowling about war, I now realized my current opportunity made me an ambassador to our country and this part of its history. I felt a rising sense of pride in our flag as I thought of those who served our nation to preserve our freedom. Forever in my memory would remain my visitor's words of gratitude and strong camaraderie with my dad. While he didn't personally know him, they had lived through a common era and emerged from the past with a bond obviously real. They had served their country "together."

    After walking with them to the door and saying goodbye, I came back inside. Then my eyes searched the shadows of the room cautiously, but no one was there. I felt like someone was staring at me! For the first time that summer, it was a bit eerie inside the museum, alone with those scenes from wars past.

    I looked at the World War II exhibit again and the details the old veteran had just pointed out: the plane, the guns, and the flag. I noticed the artist had depicted our American flag in every panel, either waving or still. Old Glory had a consistent presence I had previously overlooked.

    A few weeks later, another small group came through. Even though they signed the guest book by the door I had not yet determined if they were family, friends, or had entered at the same time simply by chance. Quickly, though, I learned that they knew each other. As they approached the Vietnam War scenes, one of the women began to cry, moan, and then wail loudly. The other women in the group immediately comforted her, and I realized her son had died during this war.

    I was at a loss and didn't know what to say. I remained as silent as the painted faces on the walls. The grieving mother wanted to be alone. The others honored her wishes. They approached me and inquired about how to make a monetary donation. As I provided them with the information, they became interested in my dad's latest project—listing all the names of those killed in action. Just as I was giving the details, Dad arrived and the group stayed for another hour talking to him. The mother of the deceased Vietnam soldier hugged my dad as she left and thanked him repeatedly for his efforts to honor all the soldiers in our history.

The next afternoon I sat alone at my boring job, once again surrounded by the painted faces of soldiers I never knew. However, I finally understood who they were. They had fought, and some had died, so I could live in a great country with hope for freedom. The faces of my summer job experience helped me empathize with feelings of losing a loved one and taught me about sacrifice that provides freedom for all people. My dad lost his only brother in 1944 during World War II. While I knew the facts, I had never felt the pain he and my grandparents must have experienced, until forty years later when I worked that part-time summer job.

This opportunity allowed me to see the issue of war through the eyes of Old Glory and I now know that "real lives" and "true" describe the *red, white, and blue*. With tears and smiles, I am thankful for those who fought in all the wars to keep us safe at home, free to live our lives in a way we often take for granted.

Oh Lord, humble us to remember; help us to realize the price of sacrifice; hold us to honor you for the many blessings we have in America.

~ Pam I. Barnes

THE FLAG I WILL NEVER FORGET

I grew up in a house without weapons, so the loud report of a twenty-one gun salute shook me to my toes. I am rather ashamed to admit that at the age of fourteen I was not as concerned about the grieving family of Thomas Blanks as I was about the peculiar fact that I was present at his ceremonial, military funeral.

My brother's friend had been just one of many faces at our dinner table so I doubt I would have recognized Thomas Blanks if I had met him on the street. I did not know the first names of any of his many siblings, there was no story that I could recall that explained why his father was not present, and I was just guessing to place the red-faced girl next to his mother as his fiancée. I was not close to any of these people.

So what was I doing at this stranger's funeral? As far as I could determine, there must be only one reason. My brother Mike wanted me there. But why?

Stiff and remote, Mike was motionless and seemed unreal in his drab, army green uniform. He had been absent at our table for long months since being drafted into the army, and his appearance had drastically changed. With his buzz cut and unbending, frozen posture, Mike resembled a cardboard recruitment poster.

    Mike was oblivious to me during the formal military graveside service, but I decided he must have been the one who suggested I be here. My mother always tried to shelter me from the unpleasant realities of life, and I'm sure my father couldn't have cared less if I was present.

    I flinched as the guns fired on that dull, gray January afternoon. A bugle player forlornly sounded the taps as soldiers in uniform lifted the draped flag from the coffin and meticulously folded it with ceremonial precision. After thirteen folds, their pristine white-gloved hands had formed a neat triangle. With a final tuck, the careful and prescribed movements completed a plump flag pillow. There was a salute followed by the now retired-from-service American flag being marched over and presented to the deceased soldier's family.

    Mrs. Blanks sobbed as a fresh wave of anguish swept over her. A soldier handed this grieving mother a grateful country's gift. All the women, including my mother, seemed to draw nearer and huddle in close in a vain attempt to comfort her, but the poor woman would have none of them. She only wanted the hand of her second born child, now the oldest son left to her. She leaned heavily on that pale boy. I do not remember his name or his face. Just like Thomas, that boy was a stranger to me. I felt embarrassed to witness their private agony.

Scriptures were read as ragged sobs broke the silence; an unnerving ambience fell over this sad assembly. I respectfully bowed my head, but I was mystified by this extraordinary change of mood. Something was being said about how trials developed one's faith and how we should seek the wisdom of God when we did not understand pain in our lives. With one eye in a squint, I peeked at the one person I trusted to never laugh when I asked about perplexing, adult concepts—my brother Mike.

I keenly observed how Mike was reacting to the crying and desolation as the soldiers turned a hand crank to lower the gunmetal gray coffin into a huge hole in the frozen ground. I was surprised to discover that Mike did not have his head bowed. He was not even looking at the gravesite. His gaze was locked far off into the distance. At first, I thought he was staring in shock, but after I traced the path of his vision, I realized he was enraptured by an object flapping in the icy wind.

Never before or since have I witnessed an American flag wave like that one. Far across the field, past the many grave markers, the flag snapped with each chilly blast. The demons of the air seemed determined to rip that flag from its high post, but it held firm. With chain clanking against its metal pole, that flag struggled with every thread of its being to maintain its grasp. I decided that it was God Himself holding back this assault on that flag. As it desperately held on in the tortuous wind, it proudly presided over the cemetery.

I stepped closer to my brother and hovered in Mike's shadow. Though still saluting at military attention, he reached out to me. His wife was nearby, our parents were close, and there were friends all around, but it was my hand he held. My brother, who usually shunned such touchy closeness, squeezed my hand in reassurance.

Mike, who had never been comfortable articulating his feelings, was especially inept in explaining to me why he was going away to the same war that had taken his friend's life. I needed him to somehow make clear his confusing reasons, and his determination to serve this intangible barrier between his home and the other pockets of peace in this harsh, unforgiving world.

Maybe only I yearned to understand what he was doing. I know he was passing to me something exceedingly important about life. By being at that gravesite together, he needed me to understand. We shared what God used to bond a brother to a sister's heart.

Just like that flag, Mike was holding onto a slim hope. He was holding onto the idea that there was something decent and good left in this world, something worth protecting. Now he was personalizing that hope by sharing with me the profound belief that protecting our freedom was often something bought at a very great price.

Trembling in the cold beside this determined soldier, I knew at last why I had been invited to attend the funeral of my brother's friend. For me, the American flag is no longer that limp cloth hanging in the corner at parent-teacher meetings.

Nor is it that distant blur that singers address at sports stadiums. It is not even that tear-soaked triangle bundled into a grieving woman's arms. The flag burned into my memory will forever be the one that valiantly struggled to persevere in the face of chilly, winter blasts the day they buried my brother's good friend, Sergeant Thomas Lee Blanks.

My brother, James Michael Anderson, lived until his fifty-third year. I cannot prove it, but I always believed that his fatal illness was aggravated by the deadly exposures in the Vietnam War. Before his death, he made a pilgrimage to visit the Vietnam War Memorial in Washington, D.C. to thank his friends for their ultimate service to our country. I visited our nation's capital and placed my hand over the name of Thomas Blanks. I said my own thank you to him that day for keeping our country free.

~ Cheryl Anderson Davis

THE UNIFORM

The rhythmic sounds reverberated off the smooth surfaces of glass and steel, ascending from street level and quickly rising unobstructed toward the summer sky. Cocooned in a skyscraper canyon, the percussion settled down heavily on us like a musical shroud. Returning from its journey, the sound waves entered my body, causing my lungs to vibrate from the impact. I caught my breath as I trembled with excitement and allowed it to set the timing for my inexperienced nine-year-old feet. Overcome with a blend of anticipation and fear, we turned the corner onto downtown Chicago's famous Michigan Avenue and were greeted by thousands in the two-mile long adoring crowd.

   Between the vibrations in my lungs and sudden pride welling up in my heart, I felt as if I couldn't take my next step. I was the youngest member of my drum and bugle corps. After strong negotiations, they reluctantly agreed to my inclusion but I was met with an immediate obstacle. No uniform. And a uniform was mandatory to march in formation. They'd given the last one away and I was so slender, the smallest size they could order would have swallowed me whole.

Undaunted, I turned to my ever-capable mother and commissioned my uniform. Mom's former modeling career gave her the experience to become my personal fashion consultant and to create a uniform for me without benefit of a pattern. The beautiful work she unselfishly produced with her love, and new Singer sewing machine, amazed all of us.

The only piece of the uniform the drum corps could offer was a maroon beret with gold crown emblem gracing its right side. I would have to assemble the rest, strictly adhering to their classic style. Memorial Day was fast approaching, and Mom and I scoured local fabric houses. With measured maroon and white satin fabric, we found an unexpected white satin blouse and gold jacket we could alter, and brought them home to undergo the construction and transformation of my couture.

My older sisters were already members in the same drum corps, *The Norwood Park Imperials,* in divisions based upon age. My eldest sister was an impressive flag bearer capable of twirling a full-size flag in perfect synchronization like an ordinary baton; my other sister was a rifle bearer, whom I painfully learned to steer clear of when she practiced her spinning maneuvers and threw her rotating rifle high in the air. They had "real" uniforms with white leather marching boots, and as siblings made it a point to remind me of these facts.

Mom labored tirelessly, burning midnight oil. Seams were ripped apart as fast as they were sewn and the fittings seemed endless. I awoke the final morning to find my one-of-a-kind uniform pressed and hanging in my bedroom just in time for Memorial Day's massive parade. Better than Christmas morning, I located my weary mother and disappeared into her arms with overwhelming gratitude. I tried on her "love" for the final perfect fitting.

Our drum and bugle corps had proudly held the successive illustrious title of State Champions for numerous years. We traveled in and out of the country competing against other drum corps and consistently ranked in the top ten. As one of Chicago's darlings, we basked in the patriotic accolades. My middle sister initially carried the official city of Chicago flag in color guard formation, the second-highest honor next to carrying "Old Glory" herself.

It was an amazing experience to be part of a larger vision at such a young age, a celebration of being an American with the competitive American spirit that all citizens are free to enjoy. I was dedicated to my corps, my city, and my country as I embraced the shared experience of corporate submission with finely synchronized results. Hundreds of knees elevated simultaneously, flags tipped forward or twirled in unison, rifles spun at exacting speeds and heights, while drums and horns punctuated every maneuver. It was a flawless result evidencing the profound power in likeminded goals and vision regardless of age.

At just nine-years-old, I was placed in the front line of my corps formation. I marched in the color guard beside my faithful companion, *the American flag*. Our row was the first visual cue of the 150+ members of the marching corps behind us. As we tensely waited our turn, the music from other high school bands and drum corps wafted through the charged atmosphere. Chicagoans are famous for their elaborate parades. Every holiday marked a reason to celebrate and unveil skilled entertainment. As the most ethnically diversified city in America, Chicago had ample opportunities to showcase their represented heritages beyond the usual calendar holidays. Event planners dyed the Chicago River *green* for the annual St. Patrick's Day parade. However, our patriotic holidays were the most elaborate, often culminating with fireworks discharged in Grant Park near Buckingham Fountain overlooking beautiful Lake Michigan.

    It was a genuine honor to participate in such events. Because of the corps' elevated status, we were often the last to appear in civic parades. The emcee announced us, and his echo reached our waiting area. Instruments went up, flags lifted into their waist holders, rifles rose to steadied noses, and our beautiful American flag was hoisted high beside me, unfurling her vibrant colors, and casting a protective shadow over me. In the midst of clamor, I felt safe. Awash with patriotic pride, I quickly looked behind me for both sisters. Reassuring looks were exchanged and in unison, all 150 of us took our first step into the excited crowd.

    The Windy City lived up to her name and caught hold of Old Glory. The flag pulled hard against its bearer, displaying strength in both of them. I briefly looked down at my shoes. The salesman was right. My ordered boots missed their deadline and I was forced to wear white shoes and socks, thus becoming the proverbial sore thumb. Changing my disappointed view, I focused on Mom's artistic craftsmanship and enjoyed seeing each white satin pleat peek out from my maroon skirt every time I lifted my marching knees. The music carried me away and I was lost in the moment.

There was Dad. A permanent fixture on the sidelines, he was running backwards and snapping photos. I still don't know how he escaped years of potential injury. Camera film sales tripled with three daughters in drum corps, and Kodak's stock rocketed. I remember how excited he'd get when the slides were developed for viewing. An afternoon call home meant dinner would be early, and the evening was spent watching ourselves on screen in the dark while munching on stovetop buttered popcorn Mom served in wax paper cone containers. Just the way she'd eaten it as a child.

After marching a few blocks, eagerly scanning the crowd, while staying focused on keeping in step, I finally located the face of my dear mother, beaming as usual at the loves of her life. She was the first American born into her immigrant family and wore the title well, teaching us undying respect, love, and devotion to our country. She and I were equally blessed with my hand-made uniform and the defeated opposition it represented. It was a labor of love birthing heartfelt pride in two completely separate applications.

That Memorial Day parade was the first of many I would enjoy with participation. Numerous competitions lay before me with hours of practice, several wins, and several losses. I would spend many more nights surrounded by family against the soft glow of our slide projector and occasional cancellations of viewing due to an unexpected blown projector bulb. Laughter erupting at funny images of Dad's photographed fingers, a surprised Shriner, unique characters in the crowd, and parade horses. His pictures often taken while avoiding a fall; backwards photography had its unexpected rewards.

I am privileged to live in a country built on the American dream; built with the foundation and bricks of immigrants' courage and gritty determination. *I am a proud American,* blessed to have my flag's colors splashed across my life, protecting me and the values I treasure. My hand covers my heart without prompting when respecting my country, pledging my allegiance, and honoring my flag. A flag so sturdy and stitched together by God-ordained principles, that it can leave our shores and fly with integrity 238,857 miles into space to be planted on the surface of the moon. Often visualized through *other* countries' telescopes.

We *are* one nation under God, inviting His presence and blessings to rest here. He, too, understands stripes on His back, stars in His crown, and glory in His presence. Personally knowing this makes me a dedicated American marching in God's front line.

And to this day, when I hear a drum line sound off, that rhythm seizes my heart and I instinctively prepare to take my first step. Which isn't hard to do. My boots are still in the attic.

~ Susan M. Watkins

MY GOD MY COUNTRY

How often do Americans reflect upon the blessings we have received from our loving God? I feel very fortunate to live in this country, free from the ravages of war and oppression seen in other countries around the world. We are a peaceful people who recognize the vast blessings that God has showered upon us.

So why does God shine His glorious light so brightly on this land called the United States of America, and why do we as a people seem to have more than other countries?

I am not sure I have the answer to this question. However, I am convinced—God expects much from those who receive much. As a nation drenched in great amounts of wealth, resources, technology, talent, and opportunity, we should consider ways of giving our thanks to God for such great abundance.

One way we can do this is by sharing with others in need. We frequently provide comfort, relief, and assistance to nations who are without the most basic things, like food, shelter, clean water, and medicine; things we so often take for granted.

As a generous and compassionate nation, we have always helped God's children in need. We lead by example, taking a prominent role to provide immediate relief to our brothers and sisters in countries like Haiti. The impressive amount of resources and manpower we commit for ongoing assistance to needy people amazes me, and I am proud to say I am an American.

Now let us reflect a moment on how we give thanks to God for something so intangible as our freedom. Do we recognize how blessed we are to live in America, and understand the large amount of daily resources it takes to ensure our nation's safety and security? As we give thanks for our freedom, do we consider the American service members who devote their lives to protect us?

If we think about the word "sacrifice," as it applies to those who choose to serve in our armed forces, we might begin to comprehend why so many of our citizens volunteer to defend America's freedom, liberty, and sovereign rights. They make a conscious choice to dedicate their lives to defend and protect our nation from those who wish us harm. Are they born to be soldiers, sailors, aviators, and marines? Does our heavenly Father endow them with certain traits, attributes, and strengths? Perhaps, but I believe the true reason they don their uniforms and go into battle for our country is that they are given servant hearts. They are willing to make the ultimate sacrifice, so their families, friends, and yes, their country may continue to live with the freedoms we enjoy.

Average American citizens unite to preserve our way of life. We stand up for freedom, liberty, and the inalienable rights granted to us by Almighty God. Brave civilians have given their lives defending our country. We are America, and proud to be "one nation, under God, indivisible."

As a Christian believer and retired soldier, I am proud to serve my God and my country in many different ways. My decades of military service changed my life and made me a better man. I truly believe my military experience was something that God planned for me. I often witnessed the incredible sacrifice of honorable soldiers and their families, and I pay tribute to the many unsung, nameless heroes that most Americans rarely celebrate. They live in our communities all across this great land and they do God's work according to their call and unique life's purpose. Some serve unto death so America can remain free.

When I was a child, I imagined I might someday serve my country. I felt it when I stood to face the American flag in elementary school. My classmates and I recited the Pledge of Allegiance together and I sensed that there was a special plan for me. God has a special mission for each of us to carry out. As I matured and began to understand my calling, I was willing to go where God would send me. I trusted that He would love, guide, and protect me along my way; He always did.

I wore my uniform with pride and lived those years by faith. Then and now—loyalty, duty, respect, selfless-service, honor, integrity, and personal courage are values I share with others who serve God and country. These values live in my family and in the lives of Americans I meet every day.

I will take these values to my grave, those gifts that our loving God breathed into me at a tender young age. I will be buried with those values, dressed in a U.S. Army uniform, my dog tags and crucifix around my neck, and the American Flag draped proudly over my body.

~ Stephen Caravana

THE UGLY SOFA

The summer of 1965 began on a despondent note. I had recently graduated high school, and desperately needed a summer job before starting college that fall. We lived in a small Mississippi town. All my efforts at locating a job had been to no avail. Daddy felt I needed "help" and decided to intervene. A friend of his, Mr. Ramsey, managed a furniture manufacturing company on the outskirts of town. Over dinner one night, Daddy calmly announced, "I spoke to Mr. Ramsey today about your need for a summer job, and he said you could start work at the furniture company Monday. You'll be working with a lady who's been there for years helping her type furniture orders." He was so proud of himself—beaming actually. I, on the other hand, was horrified!

"Daddy, I can't take *that* job," I protested. "I can barely type anything without mistakes." I had taken a typing class my senior year; however, my teacher was a single, attractive young woman, fresh out of college. She wore mini skirts to school and her dark, wavy hair flowed all the way to her waist. Most of the students in her class that year were football players, and they were more interested in entertaining the cute teacher than in learning to type. We barely learned the keyboard that year.

Daddy, who would not be deterred, ordered, "I told him you would take the job, and that's exactly what you'll do. You have all weekend to brush up on your typing. You'll do fine, I'm sure." End of discussion. I resisted taking this job with every argument I could conjure up, but there was no dissuading my daddy.

I reluctantly showed up for work the following Monday. The office was a tiny refuge in the middle of the noisy chaos of the warehouse. The manager welcomed me to the office and assigned me to work with Christine, a tall, graying woman old enough to be my mother. Christine calmly explained how the orders for furniture were processed and patiently taught me how to type the codes that dictated how each piece of furniture would be made.

By the end of my first month, I couldn't honestly say that I enjoyed the job, but I had begun to relax and feel more comfortable. That is, until Christine dropped the bomb by announcing that she would be away for a week on vacation. Fear rippled through my body. How could I survive a week without her help? I immediately began sending my emergency prayers to heaven!

"Oh, you'll be just fine," she said as she patted me on the back and nonchalantly waved away my protests. "I'll be back before you miss me."

The first couple of days went smoothly enough, and they passed by quickly. Then disaster struck! The manager burst into the office, his face beet red, with his chief foreman trailing closely behind him and talking ninety miles an hour.

"I don't know how to explain that sofa. All I can tell you is that the order was made exactly as it was typed. It's not his fault."

I sank deeper into my chair, longing to hide under my desk. The manager dismissed the foreman and slammed the door to his office. As soon as I dared to move, I crept quietly out the door in search of "the sofa." I didn't have to ask where it was. It sat in the middle of the warehouse like an ugly duckling. It was hideous—armrests covered with orange flowers, cushions covered with pink checks, and backrests a shade of chartreuse that made you look away. There was no doubt in my mind who was responsible for the ugly sofa.

I went back and timidly knocked on Mr. Ramsey's door, entering when beckoned. "I couldn't help but overhear your conversation about the ugly sofa," I said. "I am so sorry. I typed the order incorrectly, and the mistake is my fault. You can take it out of my pay until it's paid for."

I knew it could cost me my entire summer wages, so I was totally taken aback by his response. "I appreciate your honesty, but that won't be necessary. The sofa can be reupholstered, and we'll have no trouble selling it. You'll see." I was thankful his temper had cooled.

A few days later, he motioned me to follow him out to the work area. We stopped in front of one of the most beautiful sofas I had ever seen, one anyone would be proud to purchase. So unsightly before, now it was upholstered in lovely, matching fabrics.

I managed to finish out the summer at the furniture plant with no other major mishaps. For some reason, though, I was never called to work there again.

~ Louise D. Flanders

OUR TRIUMPH

As children, we were inspired by many ideas of good and evil from the popular culture of the time. Our heroes were the men in white cowboy hats, superman, astronauts, and GI Joe. We watched reruns of western shows where the good guys never allowed their hats to hit the ground as they fell off horses and met evil in hand to hand combat. Super heroes inspired us to clip towels around our necks so we could run through the house with arms extended, imagining ourselves as conquerors of evil.

GI Joe was another one of our childhood heroes, and a real man's man. Unlike Ken, he didn't hang out with Barbie and her pals, but evaded my sister's attempts to play house and dress him up. He was busy with his military training, wars, and maneuvers as the general who led bags of plastic soldiers into many battles and adventures.

On one visit by my grandparents, my grandmother gave me fifty cents. I rushed to the five and dime store to buy a deluxe bag of combat reinforcements. In the bag were one hundred plastic soldiers, including five paratroopers who headed up the invasion against the unseen enemy.

From my back porch, my friends and I would launch the paratroopers high in the air and watch them float safely to the ground into enemy territory.

I was amazed at how the parachutes brought them gently to the ground. One day, the thought struck me; if plastic parachutes would work for these army men, they would work for me too. Under the kitchen sink was a pack of thirty-gallon black plastic bags. The ratio to my size looked to be about the same as the parachute on the plastic soldier, so I was sure this would work as a human parachute. I rigged it up and climbed onto the roof. I made my way to the side of the house where I would have more open space to drift down.

The weight-to-mass ratio was right to my seven-year-old mind, but my physics were slightly off. I peered over the ledge into the enemy's camp and boldly launched into the air. For a moment, time seemed to slow. The ground was approaching much too fast and I looked up to see the source of the problem. Instead of inflating, my trash bag collapsed and flapped in the wind as useless as a flag waving good-bye to the top of the house. The ground slammed into me and it felt like my ears were introduced to my pelvis. After rolling around until the pain subsided, I inventoried my body and was delighted to find I had no missing parts. From that point on, I would allow the trained plastic troopers to head up the invasion from the air.

I loved the show *Mission Impossible* because it exercised my young imagination. The agents were good guys, infiltrating the enemy's camp with stealth for a well-planned adventure. I decided that I, too, would take on the mission and find a way to sneak into an imaginary fort residing on my back porch, to overthrow the bad guys. My mission was simple, but required precision. Invisible guards were watching the ground, so I had to leap from the bathroom window to the back porch, without alerting the forces looking out for invaders.

I hung from the window, preparing for the six-foot leap to the porch. I spotted my landing zone. I would grab the banister as I planted my feet on the edge of the porch, then dart through the railing to safety. It would have worked but ... I left out an important detail. It had just stopped raining. I landed perfectly, grabbed the rail, but my shoes did not find traction. Instead, they shot forward, making me lose my grip on the rail and fall backward off the porch.

Once again, the hard ground greeted me. The momentum made me hit on the flat of my back between my shoulders and I had the wind knocked out of me. It seemed like a long time before I could draw my first breath. I don't think I ever told my parents about this incident. I could envision them giving me that "surely you aren't that stupid" look. I wish I could say that this knocked sense into me, but it would be a while before my abilities ceased to exceed my wisdom.

As children, we were impressionable, and while we had trouble separating special effects from reality, at least we had good guys as role models. Superman, the Lone Ranger, and sports heroes that valued honor in their conduct taught us that being a good guy put you on the winning side. The rifleman was shot and John Wayne was backed into a corner, but good didn't lose. When evil seemed to triumph, it was only delaying its inevitable defeat. John Wayne rallied the troops to victory, and even with all his wounds, the rifleman still managed to stagger out to intercept and defeat the gang of bandits threatening the town. When the good guy had to stand alone, it always taught the lesson—good always prevailed.

God gives us childhood experiences and our imagination to provide a glimpse into His master plan. Good continues to prevail. It is something the Lord has instilled into the heart of mankind. Whether in imagination or personal experience, victories are given to the weary to remind us that His goodness will always triumph. Even when darkness seems to surround us, we take comfort in knowing how the story ends. Whether we stand as one or alongside others, and in spite of all odds, only righteousness will ultimately remain.

Life is filled with foolish acts, some crossing into the realm of stupidity. Our inflated sense of wisdom often causes us to imagine ourselves to be heroic, like a caped child imagining himself flying as his feet remain on the ground. When we have eyes to examine ourselves honestly, we see that deep down we are all children, making decisions that seem right, but are as foolhardy as parachuting off a house with a trash bag.

The good news is that our lack of wisdom and foolish choices do not determine the final outcome. If anything, the Lord allows us to make these painful choices to show us our own limitations. Standing upon His Word is the only wise choice we can make. Hope cannot be lost when we realize that falling flat on our back is not defeat, nor does landing on our feet guarantee success. Faithfulness and obedience belong to us, but success belongs to the Lord.

We can't reverse our mistakes, but we all can stand firm on the single thing that we know is true. Those who wait on the Lord will be renewed, and God uses the foolish and weak to overcome the mighty. Be thankful that our foolishness and weakness can turn our hearts to depend on God; we are free to live, knowing that our confidence is firm, even when perfection is a distant dream. So when we jump and then say, "Oops," hope still remains. Our helmet of salvation cannot fall to the ground.

When you stop and remember the past, do not fret over lost opportunities, failed attempts, or faulty decisions. Whether remembering the history of America or our individual past, let's view those memories through faith in God's high calling.

Without pain and failure, we cannot fully appreciate joy and success. The Lord has promised that if we walk by faith, we will be without offense on the day of the Lord.

Mistakes can't nullify this promise. Instead, they point us away from self-dependence and to the firm foundation of our faith in Christ. On this, we will stand in triumph. His strength is perfected in our weakness and His wisdom overcomes our foolishness. Let us glory in our weakness as we keep our eyes on the finish line—the Author and Finisher of our faith.

~ Eddie Snipes

AMERICAN KALEIDOSCOPE

Where and when, and who and how.
There and then, and you and WOW!

High school, college,
War and peace;
Should we ever seek release?

America the beautiful; America the sane.
But have you ever noticed,
America's not to blame?

Football, baseball,
Elmer Fudd;
Apple pie,
Wynonna Judd.

All free like you and me
To think to gaze above;
And wonder at His love.

So we share what's here and there
Of what we've seen in life.
America remembered,
Our home, our joy, our life.

~ James Franklin Gardner

HOPE FOR ALL SEASONS

Many moons ago when I was just an elementary school girl, I would fling my closet doors open and spend several minutes in turmoil. After all, I had an important decision. Which pair of designer jeans, brand name sneakers, and exquisite perfume would I wear today? You see, as a student at one of the most expensive schools money could buy, I fit in just fine. A stretch limo patiently waited to shuttle me to my school's front door. My driver would stay until I had sashayed into the building. My carefree lifestyle brought me much happiness, and I plastered a smile on my face to prove it. Ah, those were the days.

From fiction to the truth—I spent my mornings gazing at hand-me-down clothes from an older cousin, big sister, neighbors, and anyone else who would contribute to my closet. On occasion, I would wear a designer outfit. The label read, "Made especially for you by Alice." Didn't everyone know my famous Aunt Alice, the community seamstress?

Sometimes I donned items carefully selected from the clearance racks of the mall stores, but more often than not, I wore my mom's hand-sewn originals, crafted with love. And wasn't a mother's love the best label a polyester cotton blend shirt could possess? Really, who needs garments with brand emblems and designer logos anyway?

    Although my mom and aunt were excellent seamstresses, they couldn't get their Singer sewing machines to spew out a pair of shoes. As a result, I usually wore inexpensive white or navy canvas sneakers that were advertised with this theme song, "Fish heads . . . they make your feet feel fine. Fish heads . . . they cost a dollar ninety-nine." Somehow, we never seemed to get upset when these shoes caused the neighborhood youth to break out in song. All the girls on the block had them at one time or another, so this childhood chant became a well-known urban anthem. I've never heard of any other brand that generated this kind of camaraderie.

    One wet, winter morning a close friend of mine walked to school wearing her fish heads. By the time she made it to our classroom, she was shivering all over. It took only one glance at her feet for all of us girls to empathize with her. What a dilemma! Most of us knew better than to wear those thin cloth sneakers in such weather.

    Once our teacher, Miss Smith, got a glimpse of this student's drenched canvas kicks, she sent her back home to change into an alternate pair of shoes. It only took her about twenty minutes to return, warmer, and drier. Even though my classmates and I knew fish heads didn't always make our feet feel fine, we sang the song at every opportunity.

    Catchy tunes were big back then. A TV jingle for a popular perfume remains chiseled in my memories. However, such luxurious scents rarely graced my pressure points, unless I spotted a tester bottle at a department store counter and bolted over to try some on. Typically, I purchased one of the fragrances sold by an Avon sales rep. I often bought the discounted items listed in the back of the catalog. They still smelled wonderful, so I didn't mind. When the order was ready for pickup, Mom would drive my sisters and me over to the Avon lady's house. We cherished our time with the woman and her cute, overweight chihuahua. An outing at the mall for an overpriced, fancy-packaged bottle of cologne simply couldn't compare.

Mom taught me how to stretch money, food, and my potential, although stretch limos never seemed to enter the equation. Oh, but a chauffeur *did* drive me to school every day—along with nearly fifty other students—in what was known as The Big Cheese (the yellow public school bus). I preferred to travel in this fashion with my friends, and it was one of the high points of my day. When parents drove their kids to school, children missed this opportunity to socialize.

I breezed through middle and high school with a "can-do" attitude. The day came to receive my high school diploma. Spritzed with discounted Avon cologne and clad in a store-bought inexpensive dress, I strutted proudly across the stage. I was sixth in my class. My sights were set on a prestigious and pricey education from a Washington, D.C. university. Without a scholarship, though, I knew I wouldn't be able to attend. Yet I was confident I would go to college. My years of obedience, patience, frugality, hard work, and purposeful contentment weren't for naught.

Not surprisingly, the Lord provided a way. He always does. I received a full scholarship to a university only fifteen minutes away from my parents' home. It included my tuition, computer, meal stipend, dorm room, and books. Our God sees, knows, and rewards.

From my upbringing, I learned to embrace my circumstances, hope for better times, and persevere. I've learned that my perception affects my attitude. I could have chosen to focus on the "have-nots" that cause some to be discontented, but I decided it was better to count my daily blessings and respond with thanks.

Nowadays, and especially during difficult circumstances, I rely on memories from my childhood, which bring a genuine smile to my face. My countenance tells others that I have hope. It shows that I know God is the one who carries me through my trials and into better times. In other words, I believe; therefore, I'll survive.

The economy gets tough, people get sick, marriages get rocky, kids become unruly, friends betray trust, and jobs become insecure. However, I've learned that God is bigger than any of these things. Through Him, I have peace, solace, wholeness, and grace beyond my wildest dreams. He understands me and calls me His own. He knows my heart and my level of effort, faith, and endurance.

Relying on Christ, I emerge a much stronger, wiser, and resilient woman. I've learned that rough times are seasonal, but I have an "all-weather" God. Consequently, I've trudged through and survived the harshest of winters with hope. I simply had to remember not to plod through them in a pair of canvas fish heads.

~ Cherise Bopape

THE CABBAGE PATCH CHRISTMAS

It was December 1983, and life was good. The celebration of the year was rapidly approaching. Along with our three girls, we had joyful hearts and excitement about the season. Our Christmas tree was up and our favorite song, "Mary Did You Know?" by Kenny Rogers and Wynonna Judd, blared loudly from our sound system.

I was engulfed with a busy schedule, working all day cutting and coloring hair at the beauty salon I owned. Any spare minute I could find was filled with shopping—I do love to shop. News commentators talked constantly about the invasion of the Cabbage Patch Kids. Reports of adults standing in long lines and starting fights with other customers just to get their hands on one of these dolls seemed so ridiculous. At first, I laughed and said to my husband, Phil, "What possesses a grown-up to fight over a toy?" Then later that week, I learned the answer.

My five-year-old was certain she would be getting her Cabbage Patch doll for Christmas. So we began to monitor every store for their daily shipment, hoping to get three of the cuddly cuties that everyone had to have this year. I stood in the freezing rain for two hours one day, but was only able to purchase one Cabbage Patch Kid. Phil, in line at yet another store, was amazed at a mob ready to fight for their rights to one or more dolls. It was madness! We needed three, and caught the determination of the crowds. Somehow, by the end of the day, we had acquired three dolls. With sighs of relief, we felt we could relax.

In the news each day, were reports of people fighting, filing lawsuits, and even traveling to other states where they paid outrageous prices for one of these little stuffed kids.

It was three days before Christmas, and Phil had one more gift to get. While at the department store, he saw a rack of merchandise coming out of the stock room. On it was a shipment of the most sought-after toy of the year—Cabbage Patch Kids. He rushed across the store and grabbed the first one he could reach. Before he could check out, two shoppers approached him and offered to pay him twice the price of the doll, which he had not even paid for yet. However, he refused to sell the treasured toy.

At home that night he told me all about it. I thought for a moment and said, "Phil, God put that in your heart for a reason. You are not a greedy man and we already have the three we need for our girls. We should pray and ask God just what his intent was for us to acquire this extra doll." After praying together, I felt a tug on my heart and told Phil I thought God wanted us to give this doll to a needy child.

The following morning I phoned a children's services group and listened as the recorded message stated they were closed for the holidays. As my heart skipped a beat I thought, *now what?* Time was running out and I knew we had to deliver this doll to some child. Returning to earnest prayer I asked, "God, what is your plan for this doll?" But like most of my questions, I didn't wait for God to answer. Instead, I picked up the phone and dialed my church. I asked our minister what I should do with this doll. "Umm," he mumbled and then with a sigh said, "I don't know of anyone. Sorry." Now what was I going to do?

Christmas Eve arrived, and we headed off to Aunt Gloria's for our family's tradition of eating, laughing, and opening packages while we celebrated the birth of our Savior. As it became dark, we all prepared to go home. We were full, satisfied, and sleepy.

Phil whispered to me, "Hey, we still have an extra kid, remember?" *Oh great*, I thought, *Why did we get in this predicament?* I closed my eyes and said, "Lord, I do not know what your plan is. We will deliver this doll to someone, but we need your guidance." Before I could give it another thought I blurted out, "Drive to the children's hospital. There will be a child who isn't able to go home for Christmas, and she will get the doll."

We agreed and decided that we would request a girl between the ages of six and twelve, imagining how much fun it would be when we saw this little girl's eyes light up at the surprise of a famous Cabbage Patch Kid. Our excitement was unexplainable. We formed our plan. I would wait in the car with our girls while Phil went in to the nurse's station to explain what we wanted to do. It seemed like forever before he came out. He shared that the nurse would locate someone to whom we could give the doll. By this time I was irritated, thinking, *How long could it possibly take? Are there children or not?* Phil went back inside the hospital, leaving me with my concerns. As I prayed, I asked the Lord, "Is this where we are supposed to be?"

Finally, Phil returned and said anxiously, "Come on. You want to go with me to give it to her, don't you?"

"Yes, of course! I am about to jump out of my skin." I was so nervous about what I would say, and wondered how I would give my offering.

Once inside, I asked, "What took so long?" The nurse explained, "There are so many children, I went to the chapel and prayed for God to show me who should receive this gift." As we rode in the elevator to the third floor, she began to tell us about the ward we would visit. There had been an outbreak of meningitis. Four children on this floor had been diagnosed with this deadly disease, and two had not made it. We followed her into a room where a tiny baby girl lay in a crib with her parents standing by her, the picture of humble souls. For a split second, I felt very disappointed. After all, this child was too young, she didn't even know it was Christmas, and she definitely wouldn't know how other children would treasure receiving a Cabbage Patch Kid. But it didn't take long for the light to dawn on the situation. The doll itself was not the gift.

The child's mother began to speak. "She's nine months old. The doctors are telling us some very scary things. If she survives, this meningitis of the blood can leave her deaf, blind, or severely brain damaged." The look on my face must have shown my fear and shock.

I reached out to touch the child's mother and realized at that precise moment why God had chosen us that night. Thirteen years ago, it had been my baby in a hospital crib. I had been told the same frightening news. Now my baby was a teenager, old enough to watch over her little sisters. I longed to hold her close, but she was downstairs, waiting for us. I hoped she knew how much her parents loved her and her sisters. Despite the danger of the disease, she had pulled through and today is a beautiful and intelligent young girl. She suffered no brain damage, no hearing loss, and her vision is perfect. My next words came easily, with grace and confidence, "Don't worry. Your baby is going to be just fine."

Once we were alone in the elevator, Phil looked at me with astonishment and asked, "How could you give her false hope? You don't know how it's going to turn out." I admitted that I didn't have the answers, but I told Phil that God made a way for this to happen tonight. He made that doll available and led us here for a purpose, perhaps to deliver a message of hope. I didn't have a clue and the words poured out before I thought them. All I knew was that this was indeed a blessing and it was a very merry Christmas.

The next morning I couldn't stand the suspense any longer. I wanted to know about the baby girl at the hospital. The first nurse I talked to on the phone explained about the privacy act, and that she couldn't give me information. I was determined, so I tried again. I called the third floor nurse's station and began explaining about our visit the night before. I could hear the tears in the nurse's voice as she told how everyone on the floor was talking about the baby's amazing turnaround. "You delivered a message that was an answer to prayer. Miraculously, the baby's health improved and the doctors allowed her parents to take her home just a few hours ago."

I have learned to be still, to listen, and watch for the assignments that God arranges. Today I accept every opportunity to serve God in His plan for His kingdom. I am grateful to say that I am both a receiver and a deliverer of His blessings.

~ Barbara Holloway

THE MAGIC POT

I don't know exactly when the magic came into our family, but I promise you it was in the form of a Sears Maid of Honor medium-weight aluminum pot. And I *had* to have it.

Three months after Mama's death, Kathy and Kenneth, my siblings, and I stood in the basement where we were beginning the difficult task of sorting through all the things she had collected over the past 25 years. It was left up to us to decide who got what and to find where the treasures were hidden.

Straight ahead of us were totes containing collections and precious scraps of our childhood. Each plastic bin had one of our names neatly printed on the wide masking tape she had used for labels. On shelves to the right were decorations for every holiday; while to the left were the wonderful fruits and vegetables she had canned, along with several varieties of jams and jellies. We divided this treasure as we reminisced; recalling how many friends and family members through the years enjoyed receiving a gift of her famous apple jelly.

Trying to appear casual, I scanned the room looking for the magic pot in which my grandmother had cooked. I felt panic begin to rise as I wondered, *what if Mama gave it to someone or worse yet sent it to the local junk store in order to make a little room?* I knew that pot had to be *somewhere* close by. There! I spied it, lying on its side in the middle of a pile of unrelated items. The magic pot seemed to call to me.

I calmly said, "Hey, there's that *old* pot (hoping that would make it less appealing) that Grandmother used to can vegetables. What should we do with that?" To my amazement, neither Kathy nor Kenneth wanted it. Quickly I said I would take it and snatched it up before either could change their minds.

To the eye, there was nothing particularly appealing about the pot. It had been used for almost 50 years—and showed the wear of each year. There wasn't a lid, a pizza pan served double-duty for that. It was 15 inches high, 18 inches across, and had a handle with a black wooden grip at the top. But to my heart, this was much more than a pot; it transported young children to magical places.

On Thanksgiving mornings when the kitchen was filled with much activity, Grandmother would turn the pot upside down and hand Kathy and me a wooden spoon. As we watched the Macy's Thanksgiving Day parade, we pretended we marched in the band and this was our drum. We were *so* excited to be part of the corps that escorted Santa as he visited from the North Pole.

Other times, Kathy and I took the pot deep into the jungle where we rescued my infant brother from wild tigers—played by our pet chihuahuas. We dropped him into the pot, each grabbed the handle, and we ran from the danger. He held on for dear life, for as you might imagine the ride wasn't a smooth one, especially since I was much taller and my sister, Kathy, was much faster. Poor Kenneth probably got more bumps and bruises from the rescue than he would have if he'd faced the ferocious tigers alone.

While all that was amazing, that type of magic only worked for small children. The real magic of the pot happened in the kitchen each summer as Grandmother and Mama prepared vegetables for the freezer. A few times each summer, we loaded up in an old Buick station wagon and headed south to the Atlanta farmer's market. Mama, Grandmother, three teenagers, and an active little boy made these trips. That car must have had expandable sides, because once we arrived at the market we didn't leave until we had a bushel each of green beans, crowder peas, okra, tomatoes, and at least six dozen ears of corn. Occasionally we added yellow crookneck squash, butter beans, and butter peas to that haul. And if we were really lucky, we left with a watermelon. The things we brought home from the market, along with the vegetables we grew in our garden, kept the magic pot busy all summer long.

After our trip to the farmer's market, our day really started. Grandmother herded Kathy, Kenneth, my cousin, Terry, and me out to the patio and gave each of us jobs to do. We shelled, snapped, husked, and silked and didn't stop until all the vegetables were ready for the kitchen.

    The hours we spent together on that patio were idyllic. We rocked in the old metal chairs or sat on the wood swing under the beech tree, working and listening as Grandmother told us story after story of her childhood and how she met Granddad. Our favorite parts were about what bad children our mothers were. She recounted the number of days in a row the girls had gotten into trouble—in comparison, we were *good kids*. Of course, in listening to the colorful stories, we learned how our mamas had learned to wield a switch with the same skill—like that of a sword fighter!

    After all our patio work was finished, Grandmother and Mama heated water in the magic pot to blanch the vegetables for freezing or to cook the tomatoes for canning. I can't remember eating any vegetables during the winter that we hadn't helped put up in the summer. It was like having the best of the fresh harvest in the middle of January. No holiday meal was ever complete without green beans, fried okra, and cream-style corn, which is still the required table fare at our family get-togethers today.

    After Grandmother died, Mama kept the magic alive with her grandchildren, letting them greet Santa as she cooked the Thanksgiving meal. She also continued to can and freeze food in the magic pot—enough for all of us, even after we married.

Kenneth and I both follow the family tradition of canning and freezing food for the coming winter months, although I don't know how his family manages since I own Grandmother's magic pot. Kathy helps me, so we share tomatoes for vegetable soup.

It's now my turn to let children take the magic pot on adventures and to teach the art of canning. I carry this mantle with honor and pride and will continue the tradition until it's time to pass the magic on to the next generation.

~ Lynn Nester

THE DAY MY DAUGHTER DANCED

"My God turns my darkness into light."
Psalm 18:28

Around the world, people heard of the tragedy in New York on September 11, 2001. On that very same day, in a little house in Acworth, Georgia, history was being written in a bathtub.

Personally, I didn't think anything good could happen on that fateful Tuesday. Like most Americans, I left work early after hearing the stunning news. Once I arrived home, I was uncertain what to do or how to react. I found myself parked in a chair that I rarely if ever sat in. Lost in concentration, I stared in disbelief at the TV set in my master bedroom.

I barely noticed as my five-year-old, Sarah, climbed onto the bed next to my chair. The images of the plane flying into the building kept playing over and over again. Each time, I silently prayed it would miss. It never did.

After a few minutes of quietly watching with me, a little girl's voice told me how sad she was that the people were in the building when it fell down. Her words startled me, bringing me back into the present. I hadn't even realized she was looking at the screen, much less following the story. *Get a grip, Dad, your little girl is watching you.*

A precious little bundle of curls and eyelashes climbed into my lap. Remembering once again that I was a father, I explained to her that some bad men had stolen some airplanes. She was worried, and wanted to know where the bad men were.

Sitting her down for a second, I told her I would be right back and ran downstairs to fetch a globe. Upon my return, she paid attention and her little eyes followed her daddy's finger as I first pointed out Georgia and then New York. She seemed to feel a little better when she saw how far away the one place was from the other. The more I thought about it, though, my fingers were only a couple of inches apart. In a little girl's eyes that was pretty close.

Remembering that some commentators were already speculating on the source of the attack, I spun the globe around and showed her where Afghanistan was located. Even illustrating the distance with my fingers helped us to realize that it was a long way from the United States.

"They won't be coming to Georgia, Sweetie," I assured her. Secretly, I prayed I was correct.

After our dinner hour, came bath time. The sound of running water temporarily drowned out the somber voices on the TV. Sarah stepped into the bubble-filled tub and I helped her open the shampoo bottle. A blended scent of lilac, apples, and soap permeated the air. As my daughter lifted her Lion King washcloth to her face, I started to leave and go back to my post in front of the TV.

In an angelic voice that I shall never forget, she announced, "I'm ready to be baptized."

I stopped dead in my tracks. There was something about the way she said it. After all those Sundays of sitting with Mommy and Daddy in "big church," I knew she had heard about heaven. More importantly, I knew she had heard about how to get there—but she was so young.

I turned around and came back into the bathroom. I asked Sarah if she knew what that meant. Looking me square in the eye, my five-year-old little girl told me that it meant she loved God with all her heart, and that she had asked Jesus to live in her heart. A smile began to creep into the corners of my mouth, and then broadly I smiled with joy—probably for the first time that day.

I rushed downstairs to find my wife, Julie. The sadness from the day's events melted from her face as I told her about what was happening in our little girl's heart upstairs. We went back upstairs together, and joined Sarah in the bathroom. For this moment, the television was thankfully forgotten.

As Julie asked Sarah what sin was, Sarah explained that it was when you did something wrong. She thought a minute, her tongue working the sides of her mouth as her mind pondered her mother's question. "Like stealing something that doesn't belong to you," she said. *Good answer.*

Julie asked Sarah what happened to her sin when she asked for forgiveness and invited Jesus into her heart. Sarah responded without hesitation, "Jesus washed all of the sins away."

Julie and I could not help but laugh. Sarah was completely naked and completely clean, in the flesh and in the spirit! We toweled off our darling, and then dressed her in her jammies. With the sound of the tub water draining in the background, Sarah, Julie, and I knelt together beside our bed. Julie lovingly asked Sarah if she would like Mommy to lead her in the prayer of salvation. As is so typical of my intelligent, headstrong little girl, Sarah politely declined, and then proceeded to pray herself. "Thank you, God, for this day, and for letting us go into your house to pray. Thank you, God, for living in my heart forever. Thank you for letting me be baptized." She wasn't finished. She proceeded to pray for the people who were in the airplane, and for the people who were in the building. Much to our surprise, she even prayed for the bad men who made it happen, asking God to make them stop. She prayed for a little boy, Joshua, who had been hit by a car, asking God to make him well so that he could walk again. Sarah had a lot on her heart that night.

After she was through, she let me pray. In that moment, which I will cherish for as long as I live, she prayed right along with me. Together, we thanked God for forgiving her sin, for letting Jesus live in her heart, and for writing her name in the Book of Life where it can never be erased.

The hugs that followed expressed celebration, relief, love, strength, family, joy, and comfort in a way that words can never describe. Sarah knew that before she could be baptized she needed to walk down the aisle at church and tell Pastor Johnny about her decision. She told us she was excited to do that, but ... her eyes lowered to the floor as her little voice trailed off. Julie and I simultaneously asked, "But what?"

"What if I am embarrassed?"

We had heard Sarah's usage of the word "embarrassed" before and knew that our daughter was talking about people "looking" at her. We told her that when Mommy was a little girl, she was shy too, but she wanted everyone to know that she was saved forever. Sarah smiled and told us that she also wanted everyone to know, so she would walk down the aisle too.

At this point, Sarah was quite finished with us. She ran downstairs and told her eight-year-old brother, Brett, that this was the happiest day of her life. Brett and Sarah hugged and began to dance a circle in the den, laughing freely as only children can. Julie and I watched this joyous scene in utter amazement.

I will always remember September 11, 2001 as the day that America was attacked by terrorists, but also as the day our baby girl danced with joy on "the happiest day of her life." The supernatural intervention of the Holy Spirit in a child's heart can happen even on one of the darkest days in our nation's history. God's perfect timing—right on time.

Thank you, God, for what only you could do on September 11, 2001.

~ G. Lee Welborn

TRIUMPHANT TRANSITIONS

The year 2001 was full of change not only in my life, but also for my family and our world. For me, there was a major transition when the minister I had worked with and supported for over four years was shifted to the senior church staff, and I did not make that move with him. The structure of our department experienced a "fruit basket" turnover, transitioning many of our staff. In ministry, we call that stretching and growing. I was *definitely* stretched—all the way to a start-up ministry offering counseling services.

Our family faced a dramatic adjustment on January 11, 2001 when my dad made a peaceful transition from this life into glory. For much of our lives Dad had attempted to prepare my sister, Linda, and me for this day by explaining that he had only asked God to let him live long enough to see his girls grow up and that anything after that was a bonus. God certainly gave our family a huge bonus because Dad was almost 85 years of age and had lived to welcome his first great-grandson.

Then in March, we experienced yet another transition from this life to eternal life when my great-aunt Sue, for whom I am named, entered heaven. She and my father were good friends and had been coworkers for a short time in their retirement years. Aunt Sue, who was six months shy of her 100th birthday when she died, was the last of her generation in our family tree. Her death moved my mom's generation to the head of the clan.

My parents were staying with Linda and her family while they were on a stateside assignment, in Kentucky. Linda and her husband John had served as medical missionaries and lived on the other side of the globe for most of our young adult years. Even though we were used to long separations from each other, we loved having them home during this time. In June of 2001, after their two daughters finished the school year, the family transitioned back to their mission work in Thailand.

After Dad's death, Linda and I encouraged Mom to apply to the mission board. She had taught us through her courageous example to pray for and financially support missionaries. We knew there had been a longing in her heart to serve God as an overseas missionary, and assured her that she had fulfilled her obligations. She had done a good job raising us and caring for our father so there was no reason why she should not follow her dream.

There was no doubt in our minds that the mission board would accept Mom, and they did! After receiving her first assignment to serve in England, the board explained a medical stipulation; she must undergo tests, including a colonoscopy, before she could leave the country. As Mom awoke from the anesthesia after her procedure, she informed the doctor that he needed to fax results to the mission board because she was traveling the next day, September 11, on a flight to England. However, the doctor informed her that she would not be going anywhere; she had cancer. In disbelief, she arranged for surgery on September 12, 2001.

Do you remember where you were on 9-11? The tragic events of this date strike a chord with all Americans. I was attending our weekly staff breakfast, and during our prayer time, someone rushed in to give us the news about the airplane attacks. We immediately transitioned our prayers to the people of our nation. America and our world would never be the same again.

At that time, my daughter, Vicky, and her husband, Jordon, lived on Long Island. Jordan's work often took him to different parts of the island, and we began to frantically call all of their phone numbers, but to no avail. Though uneasy, I remained at work for the rest of that day. I was driving to Florida later that night to be with my mom for her surgery. Linda and her family were in Thailand and I knew, because of the 9-11 attacks, they would not be able to get a flight to America if Mom's surgery did not go as well as we anticipated.

I finally arrived home to pack for my trip, and much to my relief heard Vicky's voice message telling me they were okay. I was so grateful our family had been spared.

It was an eerie drive down Interstate 75 from Georgia to Florida that night because there was no traffic passing through Atlanta. The overhead signs read, "National emergency. All airports closed." A few eighteen-wheelers were my only companions on the road. I remained riveted to the radio as they gave more details of the morning's events—the first crash into one tower, the crash into the second tower, a third crash into the Pentagon, and another in a field in Pennsylvania. *Why? What was happening?* Lots of questions with very few answers ran through my mind.

The next day, many friends and family members had gathered to pray with us before, during, and after Mom's surgery. The cancer was successfully removed, and we were told it had not penetrated the wall of the colon; thankfully, it was contained. The doctor recommended chemotherapy, but reassured us Mom would make a full recovery.

Overwhelmed with emotion, I left Mom in the hospital and headed home to pack for a previously scheduled visit with Vicky and Jordan in New York. I was comforted by the knowledge that extended family and church friends would be taking great care of Mom.

As we traveled toward New York, my husband, Michael, and I joined other vehicles inching across the bridge onto Long Island in one open lane. All other lanes were being used to remove debris from the collapse of the twin towers. We could not see ground zero, but the smoke and smell still hung thick in the air. Our entire visit was shrouded by the darkness of the horrific news clouding everything and everyone.

Later, as Mom transitioned through her chemotherapy treatments, she housed a foreign exchange student. If Mom had not agreed to be an American host for Kolja, he would have had to return to Germany. Many others were asked if they would host him, but no one was available. Mom's elder sister, Nellie, lived with Mom at the time and said, "Okay, do what you have to do." And that's how Kolja came to live with two elderly women.

Kolja moved in on a Saturday, and Mom explained to him that she was attending church the next morning, inviting him to come with her. Kolja agreed. (Later we learned he was just being polite). That morning after Sunday school, the teacher informed Mom that he had a hard time teaching the lesson because of Kolja's many questions.

When they returned home after church, Kolja and Mom spent the afternoon together as he asked more questions. Mom answered each question from the Bible, but shared with Kolja that she was not trying to make him a Christian, since no person can do that. She explained to him that only God could bring people to salvation.

The next Sunday, Kolja went back to church with Mom. That afternoon, he telephoned his parents in Germany, but since the conversation was in German, Mom had no idea what was being said. In the Sunday evening service that December 2001 night, Kolja made a public profession of his faith in Jesus Christ.

Later, at a Christmas gathering, Kolja told Mom he was sorry that she had had cancer, but that if she had gone to England in September, he might not have found the Lord. Mom's difficult transition from being healthy to having cancer, ultimately gave her one of life's greatest joys—seeing someone make life's greatest transition—from separation from God by sin to eternal life in Christ. And before the ball dropped in Times Square signaling the start of 2002, God brought another great-grandson into our family. God is good, all the time!

    Life is full of transitions—some more challenging, some easier than others. How wonderful to know God is in control of each transition in your life. No matter what, He is always with you. May all your transitions be triumphant.

~ Sue Schultz

AMERICA, HOME OF THE BRAVE

The sun sparkled that chilly morning as I rode the bus to school. I was a fifth grader at St. Mary's School. Mrs. Young, my teacher, was very old, like one of our school buildings that had been demolished the year before by a huge steel ball that hung from an eighty-foot crane. I remember how noisy it was, and how many from the parish came to watch. Despite the colossal size of the new building, the classrooms overflowed. Our class was remanded to a lone blue trailer in the middle of the parking lot. The small windows were covered with plastic and the floors creaked when we walked to the blackboard. My friends and I always volunteered to clap erasers outside so we could enjoy a bit of sun. We created a huge cloud of chalk dust that made us choke.

    Mid-morning we would line up single file and walk across the parking lot to the main building to visit the lavatory (that's what we called the bathroom back then). One particular morning, after our mid-day trip, we had hung our coats and hats on hooks at the back of the classroom and carefully slipped into our old wooden desks, trying to avoid splinters. The school secretary knocked, and opened the door. Our teacher walked over and as they talked quietly, she gasped, putting her hand over her mouth.

She waited until the secretary left, then turned to us and asked us to close our English books. Anxious thoughts welled inside as I looked around the room of 48 students. Since Mrs. Young kept a very strict schedule, we all knew this could not be good. The room was breathless as she began to speak.

"The president of the United States has just been shot," she spoke with a trembling voice. "He was in Dallas, Texas…," she pointed out Texas on the map.

"We will pray now for our president."

Over a blaring loud speaker, the entire school recited the Rosary for our fallen commander.

Later, when President Kennedy's death had been confirmed, my brother, Joe, and I mourned the loss of our favorite television shows. There were only three or four channels then but each one chronicled the news in Texas and Washington, D.C. Since that was all that was on TV, we watched the emotional drama unfold as our president lay in state. It wasn't until three-year-old John-John saluted his father's coffin on that bright fall day, that we truly joined the mourners.

But pleasant memories outweigh the bad. From 1959 until 1967, my family lived in a house with a screened-in back porch. Every spring, my mom painted the cement floor marine gray and washed the white wicker furniture. She would plump the floral pillows and the grown-ups would settle in after dinner to talk about the current times and former better days. Brothers, sisters, and cousins would play hide and seek in the backyard until well after dark, catching fireflies between games. We would come in for a treat of ice cream or watermelon and hear the grown-ups talking about national defense or economics. We were more interested in the fireflies, swimming in Scott's pool next door or heading down to the marina to ride in the boat. We didn't know about the "good old days" they missed, only that the watermelon tasted *so* good.

I enjoyed playing in my school's marching band. Our uniforms were red, white, and blue with shako helmets bearing red feather plumes. I played the fife, a small pipe-like instrument resembling a flute but with a much higher pitch. The fife and drum corps signaled the regiment to battle in the Revolutionary War and Civil War. We marched in parades all around the area. It was thrilling when the 101-member fife, drum, and bugle corps traveled to New York City to march in the 1965 Macy's Thanksgiving Day Parade. I'll never forget how cold it was that day. We wore white gloves until we had to play because our fingers would stick to the metal instruments.

A few years later, we had the opportunity to play for Senator Robert Kennedy's presidential campaign. That was just a few months before his assassination. Until that time, I had thought his brother's death an anomaly, but I quickly became aware that our nation suffered many acts of violence. After the assassinations of Dr. Martin

Luther King, Jr. and Robert F. Kennedy, sit-ins on university campuses and protests of the Vietnam War escalated. I was a senior in high school preparing for college when the National Guard shot students at Kent State. I was coming of age at a time our country seemed to be in chaos.

Regardless of the political climate, my husband and I started a family in the late 1970s and bought our first home. I remember many of my friends stating concerns over having children in the midst of such calamity. We knew America was caught in conflict, but our nation needed the support of the family unit. We worked hard, paid our bills, and on summer evenings taught our kids simple pleasures, like how to catch fireflies. Our vacations were camping trips up and down the East Coast, fishing by a quiet stream, or taking in the sights around our nation's capital. We are still in awe of the beauty and history of our country.

Our kids grew up and we traveled more. A few years ago, we hosted exchange students from other countries. While they lived in our home, we took them to Turner Field to watch a baseball game, stood by as they climbed Stone Mountain, and even took them to a professional soccer game. They were delighted with the freedoms Americans enjoy. When we sent them home, they promised to return some day to raise their own families.

I will always hold the pleasant memories above the hard times, but there are tragic events that I can never forget. One bright sunny morning, as I drove my school bus to several schools, my only care was hoping a scheduled nine o'clock meeting would be short because of my long list of errands. I had been assigned one extra run by the dispatcher that day and had missed the first report that a plane had flown into the Twin Towers in New York. When I walked in late for the meeting, I was clueless to the dramatic events unfolding across our nation.

Our director interrupted our instruction to announce, "America is in chaos, the Twin Towers in New York are no more, and several more planes have crashed into the Pentagon."

What? My mind screamed.

We sat in stunned silence as someone turned on the TV. At first, we thought what was falling out of the burning buildings was debris. Tears streamed down my face when I realized it was not building materials but people jumping out of windows to escape the fiery inferno.

It had only been three months earlier on a flight from Atlanta to LaGuardia when I motioned to the man sitting next to me and pointed out the beauty of Manhattan Island in the morning mist. The Towers loomed like a guard watching over the city. Lady Liberty stood in the sparkling waters as the swirling fog cloaked her in majesty. The man agreed that as often as he traveled he never grew tired of this sight. All seemed well with the world.

After this blow to our nation, I wondered if America would recover. We have traveled to New York three times since September 11, 2001. Each time, we see enormous progress in the rebuilding efforts around ground zero. It has been amazing.

I am convinced that the unnamed people of this nation—who work their jobs and take care of their families—keep this country strong. The firefighters, medical professionals, teachers, and moral citizens are the real heroes. America's strength and vitality is truly found within her people.

~ Patty Rocco

A TRUE SOUTHERN GENTLEMAN

"You can do it," I told myself. "Just put one foot in front of the other . . ." Once again I pushed the door open to the Alzheimer's wing. "Lord, it's you and me," I whispered.

There she was, clothes and hair disheveled, staring vacantly into space. My heart constricted each time I saw her as I grieved anew. Once an articulate geology professor, my mother could no longer converse normally. In the early days, her face would light up when I came in; we were so close. But as time went on, the spark of recognition flickered, and then died. How I missed my warm, encouraging cheerleader! All my life she had strengthened me with her vibrant, can-do personality and close walk with God. Mother had an adventurous spirit and zest for living that I loved. And her fervent prayers for me years ago when I was in rebellion had literally saved my life. I couldn't understand why God had allowed this unspeakable tragedy.

Through all the years of her illness I never found out why, but I learned how to cope by loving her unconditionally, just as she had loved me. And God sent a friend, another Winthrop Assisted

Living resident, to help me in my journey through grief.

Murphy Claxton stood over six feet tall, a gentle giant. His face radiated geniality and genuine love for people; his ready laugh and kind manner drew others to him. In the early years of Mother's illness, I would bring her with me to his room. She liked the visits. Murphy always treated Mother with respect and affection, making her feel welcome and affirmed. He was a true southern gentleman. I felt comforted to see my mother honored, despite her condition. Since gardening was a passion both Murphy and Mother shared, we would often walk together in the back courtyard admiring the flowers, and sit on the swing. Though I didn't realize it until later, Murphy started visiting Mother regularly in her wing at Winthrop.

As Mother continued to deteriorate, I often visited Murphy alone. I would leave the Alzheimer's unit with a sigh, and walk down the hall and around the corner to his room. "Come in!" he would bellow to my knock on his door, and once more I would step into the oasis. Already feeling myself relax, I would bask in his smile and sink into the sofa. At last, someone to talk to who could listen to me and show he cared. After inquiring about my family and listening intently to my concerns, Murphy would invariably talk about his family, whose pictures decorated his entertainment center. He had three children, seven grandchildren, and six great-grandchildren. He cherished them all, proudly recounting their latest accomplishments.

For all his optimism, though, Murphy understood sorrow. "I didn't have any friends," he would say, remembering his boyhood. Time and again his friends were left behind as his family moved throughout South Carolina and Georgia, following his father's business ventures. Murphy's dad would slash pine trees for their sap, mix the turpentine in his still, and then move on. During this time Murphy's twin sister died, but his parents never discussed this loss with their children. The couple divorced soon after their son left home at age sixteen.

Moving to Atlanta, Murphy sold insurance for a while, then spent the next twenty-five years with Colonial grocery stores. One day early in his career, Murphy looked up from the meat counter to find his pastor standing there. Already feeling convicted about his spiritual condition, Murphy talked with Pastor Walker further about the claims of Christ and made a decision to follow Him. He taught twelve-year-old boys in Sunday school for many years, and later on served as an interim teacher for a men's Sunday school class.

A few years after moving to Atlanta, Murphy noticed a pretty secretary at Abbott Furniture down the street. Getting up his nerve, Murphy approached her desk and asked Miss Laura if she needed any change since he was going to the bank. The best investment, they soon decided, was a life together as husband and wife.

Murphy and Laura had three children, Tony, Gary, and Becky. The family relished their mother's home cooking; Becky fondly remembers her flaky biscuits with homemade blackberry jelly. Her parents always picked the blackberries every July 4, sweltering in pants and long-sleeved shirts. Vegetable gardening was another activity Murphy delighted in. Harvesting produce from their cousin's garden as well, the family had to buy a second freezer. Later on, Murphy liked to work in his vegetable garden in Douglasville after-hours.

Offering the flavor of fresh produce, the Claxtons opened their home to friends and family for meals. The good times continued when they entertained at their Lake Lanier cabin. An old mobile home with its original pink appliances, it held "ridiculous numbers of people," according to Becky. She remembers her father driving their ski boat for hours as he gave everyone a chance to ski.

Murphy's generosity helped people in many other ways. Once, a female customer paid her debt by giving him a 12-gauge shotgun, which he promptly returned. When his brother died and left some land at Lake Lanier to Murphy, he deeded that land back to his widow. In addition, he and a friend regularly chopped wood and took it to a family in need. The best example of lavish giving was when the Claxtons took in Gary's fraternity friend, whose parents had divorced, and raised him as a son.

Generosity was only one of many qualities that attracted others to Murphy. In the grocery business and later in paint company sales, he was well-liked. Murphy worked for Armstrong Smith paint in East Point as the sales manager over several states. What a blow when his company was bought out, forcing him into early retirement. However, he called all his former customers, offered them a price list, and began his own paint business, Roadway Supply, in his basement.

    Murphy Claxton loved people, and they responded. As one of the founders of Grove Park Baptist Church, he served as a deacon, but always carried hard candy in his pockets for the children. He delighted in surprising the kids at church. One five-year-old boy in particular became his special pal, even inviting him to his birthday party. Of course, Murphy went.

    Humility characterized him, especially when his beloved wife Laura became ill with pancreatic cancer. He nursed her faithfully for five long years, taking care of her and their home. After Laura's death, Murphy continued her job of making egg custard for her 104-year-old mother. She never did know the difference.

    Murphy Claxton lived to honor God and others—a true southern gentleman. After four years at Winthrop Assisted Living in Austell, Georgia, he moved across town to Hammond Glen for a few more years. I lost my friend Murphy several months after Mother died, but I haven't lost the legacy he left. His friendship encouraged me in my journey of grief. Murphy showed me God's love in a deeper way, and motivated me in turn to pass it on.

~ Mary Bowen

THE BEST CHRISTMAS EVER

Sometimes spontaneity brings delightful surprises! It is nice to plan a vacation, look forward to it, and know where you will be sleeping; but sometimes an adventure simply evolves.

Our family gathered at our house in Alpharetta, Georgia for Christmas, like traditional Christmas times in generations past. Dave, our oldest, sat near the huge opening of the glowing fireplace, and began telling the children exciting stories of his childhood—stories about ice-skating, skiing, and sledding down "hospital hill," well known for the creek at the bottom we tried to avoid. He told of trips with the snowmobile pulling our big sled filled with the whole family and held their attention as he painted a picture of us racing down the snowy isolated roads to the Michigan National Forest. The confused deer scattered as we plowed through the forest. We would often stop and make a roaring fire for hot dog roasts and chocolate s'mores, even in temperatures of twenty degrees below zero.

The kids had lots of questions and wondered what it was like to play in snow. "How did you stay warm?" they asked. We told them about special clothing many southerners had never seen, and they were fascinated about the clothes we could plug into the power on the snowmobile.

    The more Dave described the good old days, the more homesick I became, wishing I could see my mom during the holidays. She had slipped on the ice and broken her hip in November, and was recovering in a rehab nursing home in Holland, Michigan. We all began reminiscing about our Michigan family.

    Dad had passed away two years before her fall, and it was difficult thinking about her being alone at Christmas. She was the best mom and most beautiful person I have known, loving and nurturing her family with unique kindness. I sure missed Mom.

    Dave suddenly turned and asked his wife, Lila, if she would like to drive to Michigan. She could see the excitement building. Our spouses are the levelheaded ones who would have an anxiety attack at the thought of going anywhere without a specific plan, at least a week ahead, while Dave and I are more impulsive by nature.

    Lila and my husband, Rog, both agreed they had no desire to go north, especially in the winter, but neither would mind if Dave and I took the children, who were out of school for another week. Dave had time off and I was retired, so the timing was perfect.

    "Why wait?" Dave remarked. "We can take off right after supper if we pack fast." My heart leaped with joy. Do you remember how your heart races when an adventure is about to begin? You get that great burst of adrenaline, power-packed energy, and you get things done in half the time. We quickly made a bunch of sandwiches and gathered lots of warm clothing.

"We can shop at thrift stores for anything else we might need," I chuckled gleefully.

We ate supper and away we went with four grandchildren; Dave's girls, Kristen, 11, Angie, 9, and our son Tom's boys, Mitch, 11, and Matt, 7, who were staying with us at the time, and had never gone on a vacation. The kids couldn't believe this dream was really coming true.

We didn't call anyone in Michigan to say we were coming. Mom's cozy house was empty, so we knew we could camp there. We drove all night and arrived about noon the next day, weary but happy, to find a vast blanket of fresh snow piled higher than our car. The kids could hardly contain their excitement and leaped face first into the fluffy white heaps.

The first place we wanted to go was the nursing home. When we arrived, my sister, Sal, was there helping Mom. While Mom was in the bathroom, we quietly lined up in a long row, so when she came out we could astonish her.

Was she ever surprised! My sweet mama stood there in her nightgown, leaning heavily over her walker. As her eyes inspected her dear ones, she looked down the row with her mouth hanging open. To Mom, nothing in life mattered more than her family. She was flabbergasted, and the possibility of seeing us had never crossed her mind. What a joy it was to see her again. It was worth the whole trip to make her so happy.

After a great visit, Mom fell asleep, so we went to the Salvation Army store and bought warmer clothes for the children. We found all sorts of ski equipment, mittens, and boots—the works. I was amazed at the great prices! We outfitted everyone for under $75 and even added a couple sleds.

Next the grocery store, then we settled in at Mom's. It was better than any hotel, and she even offered her car to me, which came in handy. Dave and I napped while the kids made their first snow houses and had snowball fights. It was wonderful to see the kids having such a great time.

I spent the week cooking, cleaning, visiting loved ones, especially Mom, and Dave took the kids skiing every day. It helped that my brother owned a ski store. He loaned them all skis and generously gave them free ski passes!

The Michigan cousins quickly bonded with my grandchildren. It was a special treat for me to spend time with my siblings and their families. We are blessed that our families get along so well. God's love binds us together, which is so important.

We recorded some hilarious videos of the kids skiing for the first time. They experienced some trouble trying to master the rope tow, especially after just learning how to stand on skis. This thick rope moves upward on a pulley. Skiers come close to it, grab hold, and the rope pulls them up to the crest of the hill so they can ski down. It takes coordination to line up your skis and grab on at the same time. If you fall, the person behind you falls on top of you, and like a stack of dominoes, everyone on the rope line starts falling down. If anyone gets a case of the giggles, which happens a lot, it is even harder to get back up.

Little Matt kept sliding into strangers so many times the ski patrol took him off the slope for training. It was funny to watch, but not so funny for him. However, by the end of the week he was a pro, even graduating from the bunny hill to maneuver the bigger slopes.

Since I grew up in the North, I took snow and the cold temperatures for granted. We had learned early the signs of frostbite, and knew that when our toes turned numb it was time to go in. We ate snow—but never yellow snow—and we all learned the hard way not to touch our tongues on anything metal in the winter. Taste buds take a long time to grow back!

Our vacation ended. Mom's house was spotless, the kids had become expert skiers, and Mom was healing quickly. She and I had caught up on family news. We piled into Dave's roomy van loaded with blankets and food, and headed for home.

When we got back to Georgia, the weather was in the 50's and the sun was shining brightly. It was good to be home. Dave dropped us off at our house. As we unloaded our gear, I grabbed the blankets out of the back. They were so heavy! Water flowed down on my shoes and sopped my pants. *What?* The blankets were dry when we left Michigan.

"Mitch! Matt! What is this all about?" I yelled. Mitch looked at me and started to giggle. Matt looked so forlorn. "We just wanted to take a pile of snowballs home to show our friends, Gran!" The girls appeared ready to cry. They'd had such a great time and now there was nothing for show and tell time at school—or so they thought.

"You have something even better, a fantastic video of your vacation, remember?" I said. They were excited as they agreed it was the best Christmas ever. They will never forget it and they still hope for this adventure to happen again. Maybe someday it will … but the first time is always the best.

~ Judy Parrott

WHERE ARE THE BEES?

I cherish and relish the freedom I had as a child. America, and particularly small town America, was a place for children to roam free; much like the buffalo on prairies of the past.

On days when school was not in session, each morning was the start of a new adventure. Whether it was good or bad is not in question here. I left my house in the morning, resulting in my parents not being blessed with my presence or even having knowledge of my whereabouts until I materialized for dinner that evening. On some days, when the opportunity for play was not as great, I may have stopped by home for a quick bite of lunch, if I didn't eat at a friend's house down the street.

Did my parents worry? Probably they did; but certainly not with the concern that parents have today. As a father, I know I have been extremely protective in not allowing my girls to walk, run, or play unwatched or unescorted. Of course, in their minds, this was overbearing on my part. But I keep telling them; this is not the same world where I grew up. At least they do agree with me on this point since they believe I'm from a different planet.

Watching a favorite movie, *The Sandlot,* allows me to epitomize my memories of childhood. The sound of "play ball" still echoes in my ears. Not the formal organized games so prevalent today that require regimented parental attendance, but simple ad hoc games with whomever was available on that particular day, after someone ran from house to house soliciting participants. I dare say that my parents never even knew I played ball as a child.

Was some of the play errant or aberrant? Undoubtedly it was, but not in a malicious way, rather in the creative way of children. The lack of adult supervision allowed me to do some things that in today's environment would result in the permanent loss (not just a couple of weeks) of cell phone privileges. When caught in some indiscretion on my part, punishment was swift and sure. I spent an inordinate amount of time dancing at the end of a wooden paddle or leather belt.

Play was robust, free, and almost always conducted outdoors. Inclement weather was just an excuse to get wet and muddy. We used our imagination extensively, deriving ways to pass the time. Summers were spent riding bicycles, running barefoot in the yard, and pulling honeybee stingers out of our feet. Today I rarely see a honeybee and I surely do miss them.

I routinely went swimming at a public pool and dove off a high diving board. Try to find one of those today. If I had possessed a video game, I'm not sure that I would have taken the time to play it. If I had 300 channels to watch on television, I would not have spent more time in front of the tube.

If I had a cell phone that had texting capability, messages from me would have been few and far between. My "Facebook" page would have remained faceless. Playtime was far too precious.

So what has happened to the honeybees? Pesticides, parasites, and disease have taken a toll on them. There are far fewer honeybees today than when I was a child, and almost none exist in the wild. Well-manicured lawns of fescue, zoysia, and Bermuda grass have replaced the dandelion-infested yards of the past, and the abundance of white clover on which honeybees foraged.

Even if I took off my athletic shoes today and romped through my yard barefoot, the chances of stepping on a honeybee are remote. I really miss the podiatric discomfort of having a bee stinger embedded in my foot. It's not that I enjoyed the pain, but I miss the experience that would have caused it and all of the associated activities previously mentioned. I do not recall ever having to remove a stinger from the foot of any of my children. See what they have missed!

So like the disappearance of the honeybee, the freedom known to children in the past is gone from the current American landscape. Little can be done today that is not observed. Cameras are mounted in stores, parking lots, amusement parks, businesses, and traffic lights. Technology even allows us to be observed from space.

Do I enjoy the conveniences that have resulted in this loss of personal privacy? You bet I do. It's great to be able to drive up to a machine and get money out or to instantly transfer money from my account to one halfway around the world. How nice it is to be able to call home from my car or sit at home and order some gadget while dressed in little more than my underwear.

I can hop in my car and in minutes be eating a fresh baked bagel and sipping a cup of gourmet coffee or have pizza delivered to my doorstep on a rainy, wintry night. All of these activities, wonderful though they might be, are purchased by sacrificing privacy, simplicity of life, and sometimes, I think, even sanity.

Sometimes I just want to shout, "Bring on the honeybees and the bare feet!" Freedom may be expressed in many ways and is found in various forms. My prayer is that America may always be free as a nation, but the freedom that I experienced as a child has gone the same path as the honeybees in the yard. So I'll cherish the memories and tell the stories to my children and grandchildren, so that they may vicariously experience—if only in this way—things so great about America in times past.

~ Burl McCosh

INTERVIEW WITH A SEAGULL

I woke up slowly, my mind unable to grasp the earliness of the morning, or was it morning? I couldn't figure out why my shoes had sand in them. Was I awake or dreaming?

The sand glistened in the summer heat, as waves pounded the shore. My eyes caught a quick flash above the breaking waves and I blinked, squinted, and glanced away for a moment. When I refocused I saw a seagull swoop low and proceed to climb high above the crashing waves and engineer a splash-free landing in the water not more than twenty feet in front of me. He waited only a second before taking flight again, this time heading directly toward me. I turned to avoid being hit by the large seagull and jumped when he landed just three feet away.

"That was beautiful," I said, not realizing I'd spoken out loud.

"Thank you," he replied nodding his head.

"Are you Jonathan Livingston Seagull?"

He ruffled his feathers and answered, "No, but I am one of his students."

"You've learned well."

"I'm still learning," he responded, as he glanced at my notebook. "Perhaps you have a question."

"Uh, well, yes, as a matter of fact, I do," I stammered and grabbed my pen and paper. "Please tell me, what is the most important thing you've learned as an, umm, more *progressive* thinking seagull."

He thought for a minute before answering. "You must understand that this applies to seagulls and humans as well. It is not the daily activities that *fill* your life, but rather being in constant contact with your Creator, your Teacher—that is the answer. You must have the same passion your Creator has in all that you do, no matter what it is."

My pen scribbled across the page, quickly filling the sheet with his wisdom. These were indeed words to remember.

"If you don't continue learning, you'll constantly face the same limitations you've always had. Just as a seagull is not mere bone and feathers, neither are you simply bone, muscle, and skin. You are so much more, and it is imperative that you learn and grow.

This country—from the north to the south, from east to west—was built on hard work, determination, perseverance, and faith. Without those principles operating in your everyday life, you will fail to be inspired for greater work. It is only when you cooperate with the presence of your Creator that you will understand His limitlessness *in you*. Release your inabilities and embrace His abilities. Then, you will move forward in making this country even greater.

And always remember," he said stretching his wings, "to let love and forgiveness be your cornerstones. Now, I must go." He flapped his large wings and lifted easily into flight. "Tell others. These principles are handed down from the founding fathers that helped make this country great. Embrace your Creator just as they did, and you will soar in the heavens as I do."

And with that, he flew away. I stared as he climbed higher and higher and soon blended into the vast, blue, endless sky.

Maybe I wasn't dreaming. After all this is America, the land of dreams and opportunities.

~ Charlene C. Elder

LET YOUR LIGHT SHINE

The fourth of July 2008 was an ideal day to celebrate our nation's birthday. The birds chirped, the sunlight filtered through the leaves, and breezes ruffled the lake's surface where shadow leaves danced.

We were invited to a party our neighbors were throwing and to add to the perfection of this particular day, Sherri, an old high school classmate with whom I had reconnected after forty-seven years, would be delivering a car to Atlanta and spending the night with us.

As evening approached, I eagerly watched the infrequent traffic on our road for Sherri's car. When she arrived, I introduced her to everyone then we all sat near our neighbor's dock and ate wonderful forbidden foods. Later, we gathered our crew and walked down the road to *our* lake house so we could watch the fireworks from our refurbished pontoon boat.

The twenty-year-old boat had looked to be in good condition when we purchased it. Then we removed the furniture to replace the carpet and discovered that almost everything was rotten.

Although we had practically rebuilt the boat, we were still finding things that did not work.

That night, we loaded eleven humans and one chihuahua onto the pontoon boat and cruised out to the middle of the lake. Once situated, my husband, Kerry, turned off the headlights. The stars were just beginning to come out and it was beautiful. Soon the night sky and fireworks that snaked upwards to burst like a million stars surrounded us.

Suddenly, a bright spotlight pinned us to our seats. We couldn't see who it was for a minute, but we quickly realized *it was the police.*

"You, driving the boat, let me see your driver's license," the policeman demanded.

"I don't have it with me," my husband said.

"What do you mean you don't have it?" the officer asked.

"I left my wallet on the bed when I changed clothes," Kerry explained. "I live right over there." He pointed to the closest bay.

We all nodded in unison.

The officer said sternly, "Do you know it's against the law not to have running lights on your boat at night?"

Oops, another thing on the boat that didn't work, I thought.

"And it's very dangerous to be parked out here in the dark with no lights," he continued. "Did you think people weren't going to run into you? Did you think you were immune to this danger?"

"Well, officer," Kerry said, "we bought this boat used, and everything seems to be wrong with it. I had running lights when we headed out here, but apparently when I turned off the other lights the running lights went off too."

The officer said something we couldn't hear to his partner who immediately started searching through their boat. Finally, he met with success and handed what looked like a mechanical candle to the first officer. As he turned it in his hands, it emitted a bright light that beamed 20 or 30 yards. He gave it to my oldest daughter and told her to hang over the back of the boat.

"Hold it up so people can see you," he instructed.

She muttered sarcastically, "Like I really want people to see me hanging over the end of the boat with my rear in the air. Why not bring in the paparazzi so I can be on the cover of all the tabloids. Wouldn't that be great?" She was still grumbling as we started the boat and headed for home. The police followed us until we were safely docked.

As we left the boat, my long lost friend turned to my daughter and said, "Thank you."

"For what?" she asked.

"For letting your light shine and keeping us safe," Sherri replied.

"I would never have thought of the situation that way myself," my daughter remarked. "I guess it's all in the way you look at things. That's deep. Thanks."

Just an hour ago, she had been so sassy, but now she had a pleasant smile on her face as she walked up the path to the house, humming "This Little Light of Mine."

"Way to go, little buddy," I said, as Sherri and I, arm in arm, followed my daughter up the trail.

~ Bonnie Greenwood Grant

GOD'S COUNTRY - JOE'S RESTING PLACE

After a week of rain, the air is crisp and clean. I can smell the earthy scent of the damp forest floor that surrounds this sanctuary. The Georgia National Cemetery, located in the foothills of northern Georgia, was established in 2006 by a generous and patriotic man. He donated 775 acres of prime real estate with rolling hills and scenic vistas to create a final resting place for men and women of valor who served our country in the armed forces. It is like a miniature Arlington Cemetery with uniform headstones placed with precision. Wherever you gaze you can see headstones in ordered rows, heights, and angles. And like Arlington, every soldier's resting place is honored with a Christmas wreath in December.

The Georgia National Cemetery still has large expanses of open land waiting to receive our nation's bravest. The grassy areas are manicured and framed by trees with colorful changing leaves of every autumn hue. Brilliant crimson red, shimmering orange, and golden brown leaves all seem to be praising our Creator with riotous color before falling gently to the ground on cooling breezes.

The air is so quiet that the majestic call of eagles soaring overhead may be heard echoing in the woods. As I snap photos of the surrounding beauty, I witness a deer running and leaping with grace through the center of the cemetery. She is beautiful, strong, and swift like our lives that pass all too quickly in a moment.

I feel God's presence in this place. His Word says, "The grass withers and the flowers fall, but the Word of our God stands forever." It has only been three months since we buried my brother here, but I have witnessed the first changing season, seen the withering grass and the falling leaves, and felt the unchanging truth of God's Word lift me up and give me strength. Although nature is changing all around me, the strength and peace of God's healing power is present and everlasting; His truth is a strong tower of refuge.

I love coming to this place and knowing that Joe's resting place is God's country. He would enjoy knowing that he was surrounded by nature and beauty away from the distractions, busyness, and heartaches of life. Here in this place, the glory of God is revealed and our hearts are renewed. I imagine the chorus of heaven singing, the trumpets of angels sounding, the gates of heaven opening to receive our loved ones, and God Himself collecting our tears and pouring out His healing grace upon us.

My prayer is for each of you to hear the applause of heaven cheering you on, and feel the strength of God in your lives—whatever you face today. Just as fleeting as our lives are, the troubles, challenges, and joys of life pass by too quickly.

Embrace each moment, each loved one, each pain and opportunity, each victory and joy, and celebrate the life God gave you. Each one of us is imperfect, but is perfectly loved and accepted by our awesome God. Let us love one another so that our joy may be complete.

~ Stacy O'Reilly

SEEDS OF HOPE

*Long before He guided the steps of my ancestors,
He planned my days ...*

My genealogy trails back to Native American tribes. Inquisitive about my heritage, infused with tradition and respect for this land, I feel a deep connection to these people. I often commune with God in nature settings. As I observe the splendor of His creation, I imagine the unspoiled landscapes my ancestors looked upon from lofty mountain peaks.

In old photos of these ancient ones that came before me, I can see the strength of character plainly written on their faces, not just in the strong features of high cheekbones, deep creases, and piercing eyes, but from the certain knowledge that they loved this land, each other, and our Creator.

Some of my ancestors settled along the banks of the Kanawha River in West Virginia. Located in this beautiful valley is a city rich with cultural history, the state capital, Charleston.

In 1894, my great-grandfather James Leonard "J.L." Birch took his horse and cart to the levee to pick up newcomers to this growing region. There he met passengers arriving on the big steamboats and simple barges. He was hired to transport them, their trunks, and household furnishings, often accepting an IOU or promise to pay later. Knowing how to accommodate his customers, he carefully secured their possessions for the steep ride ahead. For a modest fee, excess items could be stored until permanent housing was found.

J.L.'s business grew. When the faithful steed that had pulled the large wagon finished its days, he purchased his first truck in a line of many rigs to come. By the year 1922, local residents could phone Birch Moving and Storage at CAP 1752. The Birch family kept serving the community and eventually handled nationwide relocations. Over 100 years and four generations later, the company finally rested—but fascinating stories of my relatives continue.

During World War II years, Billy Raymond Birch, peddled produce to city dwellers from his grandfather's victory garden. He could keep 10% of what he charged. Life was simpler then, and splashing in a mud puddle or swimming at Rock Lake was among his favorite ways to enjoy life.

Once old enough, he enlisted in the United States Air Force, trained in Texas and Mississippi, and then received his shipping orders to Korea where he maintained B-26s. During his service years in the U.S., he worked on P-51s and T-33 jets.

When not in uniform, "Bill" wore leather bomber jackets, cuffed straight leg jeans, and rode a motorcycle. His family and friends were well aware of his strong will and random rebel rousing.

After his tour of duty ended, he returned to Charleston. As he sought his future, he applied for work with the owner of an automobile repair shop who told him to quit wasting his talent. He accepted that advice, used his strengths, and became employed with International Business Machines, commonly called IBM.

One fine day, this handsome and fun-loving bachelor caught the eye of a beautiful girl who was quickly moving ahead with her career plans. In those days, women had become an integral part of corporate America. It seemed fate intervened because a different man was on schedule to service the typewriters at E. I. du Pont de Nemours and Company. Mischievous Nancy Wade Crockett had intentionally jammed her typewriter. She called in a repair order, requesting a visit from a technician. Dashing Bill Birch, in his clean-cut IBM standard of crisp white shirt, dark business suit, and the newest fashion trend of clip-on ties, gallantly saved this feigned damsel in distress. He truly met his match, and that day a new chapter began in the family chronicles.

Now Bill was a young buck with a charming blend of shyness and charisma, but Nancy was a direct descendant of Davy Crockett. If you know the stories, you can imagine what that family went through with Davy's shenanigans, first as a frontiersman and later serving our country in

Congress. Young Nancy was every bit as colorful as the Disney folk hero who portrayed her ancestor.

Bill asked Nancy to be his bride. Their love story is one full of adventure that continued for over 50 years. Both served God, family, and community with big hearts. From Sunday school and church leadership to civic clubs and public safety programs, they each became involved in growing and supporting the schools and community. Concerned by adult illiteracy, Nancy taught the foundations of reading to a sixty-year-old woman.

Years ago, Nancy left for "Sweet Beulah Land," but everyone who knew her will say what an angel on earth she was. Today, Bill continues these traditions of love and service. In his veteran activities, he teaches in the community, performs in ceremonies, and serves his country proudly.

I am a branch from these two interesting folks. Born in 1960, I grew up in a suburb of Belle, West Virginia. A river park sat at the end of my street where the U.S. Army Corp of Engineers built the Kanawha River Marmet Locks and Dam. I spent many afternoons studying the activity of gates opening and closing as water levels rose and lowered in the chambers. Sitting on a grass-covered hill, I used my observation point to watch the people on the watercraft as they moved slowly through. The park offered other fun pastimes like riding bareback on Shetland ponies. One section of the park backed up to the drive-in theatre. At dusk, we watched the cartoons before the feature movie, but by dark, we were called home by our parents.

An enthusiastic adventurer, I liked to climb high up into the branches of my favorite mulberry tree. From my perch that hung far over the river, I munched on its tart berries and daydreamed about my future. There were many fruit trees in this vicinity and I can remember snacking from cherry, apple, and paw paw trees. We camped outdoors and fished in the rivers and streams of the beautiful state of our wild, wonderful West Virginia. With family and friends, I hiked up the steep mountains of the Kanawha Valley, explored caves, and ran through fields of wildflowers filled with hundreds of butterflies. I loved to create necklaces and bracelets from the tall grasses and wild clover blooms.

Mom wanted me to have grace and charm; I was happy to be just a kid. From age three, I took a variety of dancing lessons—ballet, tap, jazz, and toe, but I preferred playing football, kick the can, and our many other neighborhood games. My parents finally got me involved in Little League. But girls couldn't play football with the boys, so I became a cheerleader. From these beginnings, I developed a team spirit and went on to participate in many group performances, competitions, and recitals.

I loved my youth group and summer church camps where I gathered with others for fellowship, worship, and Bible study. We called ourselves "The Pathfinders." While God planted seeds of hope in me for His higher purpose, I learned to lean *not* on my own understanding but to trust in Him. Even now, as my world keeps changing, He remains my constant Comforter.

A vivid memory of my youth was the day before my ninth birthday, when NASA launched Apollo 11 into outer space. The team of American astronauts—Neil Armstrong, Michael Collins, and "Buzz" Aldrin—made history with this mission. While Collins orbited in the command module, *Columbia*, Aldrin landed the lunar module, *Eagle*, and Armstrong took the first human step on the moon. On July 20, 1969, Aldrin radioed earth: "I'd like to take this opportunity to ask every person listening in, whoever and wherever they may be, to pause for a moment and contemplate the events of the past few hours, and to give thanks in his or her own way." He had brought a kit, blessed and prepared by his home church pastor, and took a private communion.

We watched on TV and saw the American flag planted on the crater-filled, desolate surface. Also left behind, in the dusty regolith soil, were our Christian brothers' footprints. I can remember the tense moments of the black out period while everyone waited for the space capsule to reenter the earth's atmosphere and the celebration that followed when it splashed down safely near Wake Island in the Pacific Ocean off the shores of Hawaii. This week in history was "far out," literally, and an example of these bizarre times.

It was an era of *anything goes*.

American fads included platform shoes, hip huggers with gigantic bell-bottom hems, hot pants, go-go boots, tank tops, and beads.

People took advantage of their right to free speech, frustrating the moral conscience of America. Through inexpensive bumper stickers and iron-on T-shirt decals, sayings and images of this movement varied as widely as the decorating trends of lava lamps, shag carpet, psychedelics, smiley faces, peace signs, and black lights.

Women made strong choices about their rights, careers, and ownership of their bodies. They might wear a mini skirt one day and an ankle-length maxi dress the next. Individuality catapulted. The dress code in the workplace dramatically changed. Women wore the popular trouser suit, and men took bold fashion liberties with the polyester leisure suit in every color of the rainbow.

Always a keen observer of life, I appreciate its diversity and learn from my experiences. Back in elementary school when I was on the safety patrol, my favorite job was hoisting the American flag up the flagpole. My musical foundation was set to the tick-tock of the metronome. I joined each of my school bands, marched in the majorette corps, and learned to play many instruments. We funded our trips to competitions, festivals, and parades by selling Florida Indian River fruit and a lot of bake sales and car washes. One time we were invited to perform in the Walt Disney World Parade. Another memory is of a presidential visit to our state. Our award-winning band was selected to greet President Jimmy Carter, which we did with great fanfare when his plane landed at our small airport on top of a mountain in Charleston, West Virginia.

Life went on … and like each of you, I savor my memories of the great times we've had in America. Anticipating a bright future, those seeds of hope God planted deep within me are spouting, growing steadily toward the light. I look forward to tomorrow, assured that our Lord Jesus is leading us on the path He planned so long ago.

~ Lynn B. Pugh

ABOUT OUR AUTHORS

M. L. "Mike" Anderson is a contributing writer for several magazines. His work appears in four anthologies previous published by the Christian Authors Guild. Mike is a charter member of CAG, past president and treasurer, and is currently serving on the leadership team as our Webmaster. He formerly worked for Standard Publishing and the Parable Group of Christian bookstores. Mike and his wife, Kathy, are wild bird experts and participate in seminars and trade shows throughout the country.

Diana J. Baker is a freelance writer, editor, musician, composer, and an avid collector. Her fiction and nonfiction stories and articles have appeared in *Focus on the Family* publications, *Christian Living*, *The Wave*, and compilation books. Diana and Larry, her husband of 41 years, have pastored Prayer and Praise Christian Fellowship in Woodstock, Georgia for the past 30 years. Diana has served the Christian Authors Guild as president, historian, hospitality chair, and special projects director.

Pam I. Barnes has taught a series of classes about famous authors, "The Person Behind the Pen." She is employed by Kennesaw State University and holds a B.S. degree in marketing from Jacksonville State University. Pam's Christian fiction and poetry is published in *Heartfelt Inspirations* and *The Wave*. She is the current publicist for the Christian Authors Guild and a previous conference director. Her greatest joy is being "Mom" to two dog-babies, Bogey and Sadie.

ABOUT OUR AUTHORS

Marcus Beavers served as a field artillery officer in the U.S. Army, and then traveled for ten months in Europe. He earned multiple degrees from Georgia Military Academy and Georgia State University and worked in real estate. In later years, Marcus traveled to India, Bhutan, and Nepal. He is a past chaplain and the current membership director for Christian Authors Guild and his writing appears in five anthologies. Presently, he is working to complete a novel-length adventure. Marcus is married and has three sons.

Judy Becker, a Methodist PK (preacher's kid), grew up throughout West Virginia. After years of study, Judy published her first book, *Rightly Dividing the Book of Revelation* (2004). She then began a fiction series including *The Beginning of the End* (2008) and *The Sign of the End* (2010). Christian Television Network (CTN) interviews are on her J. E. Becker Web site. In Christian Authors Guild, Judy held leadership positions, won a writing contest, and was published in *The Wave* and several compilation books.

Nadine Blyseth, a retired teacher who lives in Rome, Georgia, never knew she had anything to say on paper. However, after her husband retired from the military and their five adopted kids grew up, she began to recall many unique characters from Alaska, Japan, the Philippines, Haiti, Brazil, and a maximum-security prison. Four years ago, Nadine began to tell their stories. Two have won contests and several have been published. She is working on an inspirational novel.

ABOUT OUR AUTHORS

Cherise Bopape lives in an Atlanta suburb with her husband and three children. With focus on her talents, she enjoys sharing relatable, homespun stories. She has written for *The Lookout* magazine and Mustard Seed Ministries. Cherise's devotional book, *Lessons from the Littlest*, afforded her a guest spot on *The Harvest Show* and other TV and radio programs. She writes a blog to inspire single moms. Cherise serves on the advisory board for a nonprofit organization that assists unwed mothers.

Mary Bowen works as an editor with the North American Mission Board and previously edited for *Witness Breakthrough* and *Walk Thru the Bible*. She holds a master's degree in journalism and writes for *On Mission* magazine. Her work appears in *Stories of Hope*, *The Banner*, *Christian Devotions* Web site, *The Wave*, and other publications. She is secretary of the Christian Authors Guild and a writing contest winner. Mary enjoys her family, book clubs, Bible study, church choir, and aerobics.

Stephen Caravana is a singer/songwriter, published author, retired major in the Army Reserve, health care professional, and founder of Vineyard Sound Books, a Christian publishing company in Massachusetts. His books *Light Beyond the Storm–Overcoming Life's Tragedies Through Faith* and *What Shall We Do With This Life–God has the Answer* shed light on God's presence in our everyday lives. Stephen enjoys spending time with his family, coaching his two sons' soccer and baseball teams, and relaxing by the ocean.

ABOUT OUR AUTHORS

Cheryl Anderson Davis, a native of Atlanta, celebrates her Southern and Celtic heritage by writing historical fiction. She won her publisher's Best Historical Fiction Award for "Hope Is Constant," a story about the American Revolution in Georgia. "The Flag I Will Never Forget," is an excerpt from her book, *Profound Thoughts*, a semi-autobiographical tale of growing up as a Southerner in the turbulent 1960s. Cheryl's work also appears in *No Small Miracles* and *Heartfelt Inspirations*.

Charlene Elder, a grandmother of three, began her writing career when first published in high school. While raising two children, she and her husband wrote and edited a national magazine, *The Salt Shaker*. Charlene writes in various genres—fiction short stories, nonfiction articles, children's stories, and poetry. She is an award-winning author and held leadership roles in the Christian Authors Guild. Her work appears in a variety of publications, including *The Wave* and several anthologies. She enjoys crafts, cake decorating, and hiking with her husband of 36 years.

Jack Elder is a freelance writer residing in Woodstock, Georgia. He enjoys writing historical fiction, westerns, diet and health, mystery, and inspirational nonfiction. In his writing ventures, Jack has written numerous Bible study courses and pamphlets. He is a past editor of *The Salt Shaker* and *The Wave,* and a contributing writer for Christian Author Guild books. He has served in multiple leadership positions with CAG. Jack is retired from the rigors of corporate work and likes reading, hiking, and traveling with his wife.

ABOUT OUR AUTHORS

Louise D. Flanders is a wife, mother, and grandmother. She previously worked as a procedures writer, and today enjoys writing magazine articles and devotionals. Her work appears in Gary Chapman's *Love is a Verb*, *Heartfelt Inspirations*, *The Wave*, and local newspapers and magazines. For Christian Authors Guild she is an award-winning writer and past secretary. Louise attends a writing conference every year and recently completed her first nonfiction book titled *I'll See You in the Morning*.

James Franklin Gardner is published in *The Fayette Daily News*, *Military* magazine, *Quantum Muse*, and *The Wave*. He was a professional pilot for 37 years, a Sidewinder 4 in the Vietnam War, and is now ordained in the Charismatic Episcopal Church. "Jim" has held different leadership positions in Christian Authors Guild, including publicity director. Jim gives all praise to Jesus as he is blessed to be the husband of one wife, a father of three, and grandfather of three.

Bonnie Greenwood Grant is a writer, photographer, and wood carver. Her book, *Carving Carousel Animals*, illustrates her passion and talent. Bonnie carved four of the thirty-three animals on the endangered species carousel at the Chattanooga Zoo. In her novels, *Run for Your Life* and *Home Coming*, she enjoys using humor to illustrate Christian concepts. In Christian Authors Guild, Bonnie participates in a writer's critique group, has held leadership roles, and her work is published in three anthologies.

ABOUT OUR AUTHORS

Linda Hayes and her husband, Dick, have three grown children. They established Herald Ministries in 1978 to equip believers through Bible studies, seminars, retreats, and teaching materials. After mission work in Haiti, Linda earned three degrees. Her writing reveals a loving Father and redeeming Savior who desire to be an integral part of our everyday life. An ordained minister, Linda shares the Word of God in a practical manner helping Christians transform challenges into victories.

Barbara Holloway is an Atlanta native who began journaling real-life stories at age 16, secretly dreaming of becoming a best-selling author. She married her military hero and embarked upon a successful career as a hairdresser. Blessed with three daughters, Barbara is now a proud grandmother of seven. A bit of a rebel, she refuses to be "boxed in" and loves the outdoors, riding motorcycles, and traveling with friends.

Toni Kiriakopoulous grew up in New York then moved to Florida to work for *The Sun-Sentinel* newspaper. Now retired, she resides in Georgia. Two of her three children are living. Toni is writing a book about her deceased son Peter. She has twelve grandchildren and is now a great-grandmother. She teaches Sunday school and helps at a Christian school. Her primary writing style is inspirational nonfiction and her work appears in *Heartfelt Inspirations*. She enjoys gardening, painting, and crosswords.

ABOUT OUR AUTHORS

William C. "Bill" Larmore began his education in a one-room schoolhouse and later served in the USAAF during WWII. He married Ava Eloise Owens and they have four children, three grandchildren, and eight great-grandchildren. Bill retired from Lockheed Marietta as an engineering artist and editor. He has served the Lord in many roles including Sunday school teacher, deacon, and mentor. He continues to be the most frequently published author in our writing group with fiction and nonfiction articles, poetry, and several books. His newest book is titled *The Distant Shore*.

Burl McCosh has written numerous poems and gospel songs and routinely wrote testimonial articles published in *Christian Living* magazine. The primary purpose of his writing is to express entertaining ideas in a clean and wholesome fashion. Burl, his lovely wife Shelly, and three daughters, reside in Marietta, Georgia. They are active in the ministry of Shiloh Hills Baptist Church in Kennesaw, Georgia. Fishing is one of this author's favorite ways to relax.

Lynn Nester enjoys writing about God's presence in her everyday life. She earned her B.S. from the University of Tennessee and master's degree in adult education from New Orleans Baptist Theological Seminary. She lives with her husband of 26 years in Marietta, Georgia. Together they enjoy travel, hiking, and time with friends. She also enjoys cooking new recipes, sewing for her home, and needlecrafts. Her first devotion was published by *Christian Devotions* Web site.

ABOUT OUR AUTHORS

Stacy O'Reilly, originally from Austintown, Ohio, now lives in Woodstock, Georgia. She graduated with a B.S. degree in Communications from Kennesaw State University where her son, Brian, now attends as a Modern Language and Culture major. Stacy is a special events planner for the Tommy Nobis Center in Marietta, Georgia. She enjoys writing inspirational nonfiction, spending quality time with family and friends, and traveling nationwide and abroad. A current special "pet" project is training her new Australian shepherd puppy.

June Parks is a true daughter of the South. Originally from Griffin, Georgia, June is a mother of four and proud grandmother of five. She is a Realtor with New Day Realty and has worked in this industry for twenty-nine years. June writes memoirs and nonfiction with humor, as she chronicles favorite stories of her childhood and incomparable family. Her work appears in *The Wave, Heartfelt Inspirations, Brush Brooms and Straw Ticks,* and other publications.

Judy Parrott writes mainly nonfiction miracle stories. Some are published and others can be enjoyed on her *Amazing Moments* Web site. She married her sweetheart, Roger, and they have three sons, eight grandchildren, and four great-grandchildren. She has shared the gospel over the years with the Christian Motorcyclists Association, taught Sunday school, and volunteered with several organizations. Judy worked as a nurse and studies to complete a seminary degree. Jesus Christ is her most important Friend.

ABOUT OUR AUTHORS

Beverly Powell is a native Georgian. She has two sons and one grand daughter, Anna, who she enjoys spending quality time with. Writing with variety—poetry, articles, short stories, and devotionals, she hopes to inspire others to grow in the Lord and accept His unfailing love and constant presence. Beverly is an addiction counselor and DUI Instructor. She teaches at her church, Mt. Paran North, located in Marietta, Georgia and also enjoys ballroom and swing dancing and going to the beach.

Lynn B. Pugh and her husband, Rick, live in Marietta, Georgia. She has won several awards for her writing, editing, and business accomplishments. Lynn likes to participate in team-building projects. She was a guest judge for Word of Life Student Ministries teen writing contest, past editor of *The Wave*, and is currently the special projects director for Christian Authors Guild. She is the managing editor of a Christian-oriented book publisher. Lynn enjoys spending time with family and friends, gardening, and creative cooking.

Patty Rocco is a Northern transplant who loves living in the South. She resides in Acworth, Georgia with her husband, John, and two rescued mutts. Her work is published in *Heartfelt Inspirations* and *The Wave*. Patty has won multiple fiction and nonfiction writing awards. She leads an inductive Bible study at North Star Church and is working on a uniting Bible study for two international ministries, Women's League and Lead Like Jesus. Patty is a previous chaplain and current treasurer for the Christian Authors Guild.

ABOUT OUR AUTHORS

Sue Schultz is a new member who attended our annual writer's conference. Her heart was captured by the keynote speaker's challenge to be a "word carrier for our generation." She is working to complete her ministry certificate through the New Orleans Baptist Theological Seminary. Sue leads the mission partnership with Poland at her church, and enjoys sharing Christ with others through object lessons and drama talks. She is married, has three children, and eight grandchildren.

Cynthia L. Simmons taught as a home school mother and Bible teacher for over twenty years. For Christian Authors Guild, "Cindy" is on the current leadership team, a past president, a writing workshop instructor, and published in the group's newsletter and anthologies. She writes both historical fiction and nonfiction for a variety of publications. While promoting her first book, *Struggles and Triumphs* (2008), she was interviewed by radio and television shows throughout America and nominated for Georgia Author of the Year.

Eddie Snipes has served as a teacher and pastor for over 30 years, including prison and homeless ministry. He considers writing an extension of his calling as he communicates messages of truth. Eddie enjoys writing contests. In competition with some of the best, Eddie won in both fiction and nonfiction categories. A favorite scripture is Proverbs 2. It is a road map of both ministry and personal growth. Eddie is happily married and the father of five children.

ABOUT OUR AUTHORS

Martha Morgan Ureke has four children and four grandchildren. She is a member of the Windy Hill Hospital Pulmonary Rehabilitation group in Smyrna, Georgia and is their newsletter editor. Martha is a member of Transfiguration Roman Catholic Church, Marietta, Georgia; cofounder/member of TAU Secular Franciscan Order (SFO) in Herndon, Virginia, and past editor of the SFO monthly newsletter. Her poetry is published in *Pulmonary Paper* magazine, *WellStar Employee Newspaper*, and *The Wave*. Martha enjoys crocheting and computer scrabble.

Susan M. Watkins, award-winning author and scriptwriter, formerly wrote for *The 700 Club* television show. Her work appears in *The One Year Life Verse Devotional, Heartfelt Inspirations, Praying From the Heart, The Wave, The Atlanta Journal-Constitution,* and various corporate newsletters. She is a columnist for a professional writer's e-newsletter with several of her stories published within that venue. A two-time winner of the prestigious 75th and 78th Annual Writer's Digest Writing Competitions; expanding avenues await her arrival.

G. Lee Welborn is a partner at the law firm of Downey & Cleveland in Marietta, Georgia where he has worked for over twenty years. He writes legal briefs by day and creative stories for fun at night. Lee is a deacon and first grade Sunday school teacher at First Baptist Church of Woodstock. His wife, Julie, is pursuing a black belt in taekwondo, and they have three teenagers living at home. Lee enjoys his role as sports announcer for the Allatoona Buccaneers football team.

We hope you enjoyed this quality book
by the Christian Authors Guild.

To view our other publications
www.ChristianAuthorsGuild.org

Proudly printed
in the United States of America

Published by

Vineyard Sound Books
Dartmouth, Massachusetts
Plotting a Course for Success

To order additional copies
www.VineyardSoundBooks.com

$18.99
ISBN 978-0-9825075-4-4
51899>